UNSOLVED SERIAL KILLERS

10 MORE FRIGHTENING TRUE CRIME CASES OF
UNIDENTIFIED SERIAL KILLERS

(THE ONE'S YOU'VE NEVER HEARD OF)

VOLUME 4

Written by
D. R. WERNER

© **Copyright 2022 - All rights reserved.**

The content contained within this book may not be reproduced, duplicated, or transmitted without direct written permission from the author or the publisher.

Under no circumstances will any blame or legal responsibility be held against the publisher, or author, for any damages, reparation, or monetary loss due to the information contained within this book, either directly or indirectly.

Legal Notice:

This book is copyright protected. It is only for personal use. You cannot amend, distribute, sell, use, quote, or paraphrase any part, or the content within this book, without the author or publisher's permission.

Disclaimer Notice:

Please note that the information contained within this document is for educational and entertainment purposes only. All effort has been executed to present accurate, up-to-date, reliable, complete information. No warranties of any kind are declared or implied. Readers acknowledge that the author is not rendering legal, financial, medical, or professional advice. The content within this book has been derived from various sources. Please consult a licensed professional before attempting any techniques outlined in this book.

By reading this document, the reader agrees that under no circumstances is the author responsible for any losses, direct or indirect, that are incurred due to the use of the information in this document, including, but not limited to, errors, omissions, or inaccuracies.

CONTENTS

Introduction   5

1. The Colonial Parkway Murders   7
2. The Oakland County Child Killer   29
3. The Disappeared of Isère   47
4. The B1 Butcher   61
5. The Eastbound Strangler   75
6. The Paraquat Killer   87
7. The Mad Butcher of Kingsbury Run   103
8. The Belize Ripper   121
9. The Łódź Gay Murders   135
10. The Family Murders   151

Conclusion   167
References   171

INTRODUCTION

Where there is life, there is also death. That obviously holds true if you think about the circle of life itself, but the living ensures death on a regular basis. Whether by predators hunting prey or soldiers fighting in a war, every living thing carries within itself the capacity to end a life.

They have their reasons: to live, to eat, to settle disputes and to punish injustice. But what if there is no reason? What if certain people out there kill just for the sake of killing?

Worse than that, what if they kill because they enjoy it? What if they kill because they see the power they have over the life and death of people, and it both thrills and gratifies their unholy desires?

With a passion for true crime and an insatiable curiosity about the minds and methods of the serial killer, D.R. Werner is a successful multimedia artist from Dallas, Texas, and an aficionado of frightening mysteries. His research into the extremely violent cases of brutal slayings around the world is fueled by a keen desire to unearth the how's, the who's, and the why's behind the most depraved incidents of murder in history, and certainly the ones that have yet to be solved. His insights into the warped minds behind such brutal slayings provide the kind of knowledge and expertise that will satiate the curiosity of those seeking answers to these mysteries.

Presenting the fourth volume in tales of the depraved and the unforgiving, this is Unsolved Serial Killers–Volume 4.

THE COLONIAL PARKWAY MURDERS

There is something to be said for the wide-open spaces of the United States that makes it both a beautiful place to visit and simultaneously a potentially terrifying one. Tourists driving through the area know that they are in for a treat as they breeze through the natural scenic beauty, meandering through forests, riverbanks, mountains, and expansive countryside. Tourists and locals alike would be wise to be on the lookout for natural traps such as ditches and the various roaming wildlife that could pose a threat to them. Nevertheless, the area also provides the perfect setting for a different kind of threat—an altogether lethal one that lurks and waits patiently for unsuspecting travelers.

I'm speaking, of course, about the Colonial Parkway Murders, a series of heinous killings that took place in the late 1980s that scarred the majestic beauty of Virginia's Historic Triangle. Eight unsuspecting victims, young men and women alike, were either found dead or remain missing to this day while their killer has never been identified.

The Method

In all of the Colonial Parkway Murders, each incident would included two victims who were romantically involved, with the exception of the final murder. They were all seen publicly by eyewitnesses, most of them friends, and had taken off in their cars toward the parkway where their vehicles were found the next day. The emerging pattern immediately indicated the work of a serial killer, as did the complexity and patience exhibited by the killer in carrying out these murders. Apart from that, the killer seemed to have a tremendous geographic knowledge of the surrounding areas, particularly those that were known for being lover's lanes. Because the murders took place in varying locations that were still in close proximity, it was difficult for the authorities to stake out potential murder sites. This was made even more difficult considering that all four incidents took place at least a year apart from each other. Different methods such as strangulation, decapitation, stabbing, and gunshot wounds were employed in the murders, but there seemed to be no evidence of sexual assault carried out on the victims.

The Victims

Cathleen Thomas and Rebecca Ann Dowski

It all began on October 12, 1986, when the authorities were informed of a white 1980 Honda Civic that was parked near the York River by the Colonial Parkway. The first person on the scene, a jogger, was running along the embankments when he came upon the car. Once he got closer, he was shocked at the grisly scene inside the vehicle.

When the authorities arrived, they were not prepared for what they would find. Since the car was wedged deep into the bushes, they were forced to smash the back window to witness the horrific sight for themselves. Once they were able to see that the people inside the vehicle were not alive, they took several photographs before towing the car back up to the road.

Two bodies, both women, were found mangled inside the Civic and had suffered a great deal before their deaths. They both appeared to have been strangled and had their throats slashed, but the autopsies were inconclusive about whether the cause of death was due to strangulation or near decapitation. Their necks and wrists also showed signs of rope burns, but there were no signs of any sexual assault, and the victims were fully clothed.

This was unlike the usual crimes of passion or those typically committed by serial killers, especially considering that both victims were young women. Robbery was ruled out as their purses were present in the car, and the cash inside was undisturbed. Examinations also revealed that while the victims may have struggled somewhat, there were no clear indicators that they had tried to fight their way out of the situation. Moreover, their bodies appeared to have been doused in diesel. However, the killer seemed to have made the mistake of thinking that diesel ignites just like gasoline, though it doesn't, as several spent matches were found in the car.

Since the bodies had not been burned, they were found intact along with other evidence.

Regardless of the brutality, the victims were identified easily as 27-year-old Cathleen Marian Thomas and 21-year-old Rebecca Ann Dowski, as their I.D.s were found on the car floor. Thomas was based in Norfolk, Virginia, and was working as a stockbroker, while Dowski was living in Williamsburg studying at the College of William and Mary, where she was majoring in Business Management. At the time of their disappearance and murders, they were dating and were last seen at a computer lab on the evening of October 9, 1986, by a friend who was with them. No one saw them again until three days later when their bodies were found.

Initially, their murder appeared to be a hate crime based on the fact that they were in a lesbian relationship. Furthermore, shortly before her murder, Thomas had resigned from the U.S. Navy as she had been investigated regarding her sexuality by nine agents. At the time, the Navy had a blanket ban on gays and lesbians joining, but Thomas had not yet realized her sexual orientation in 1981 when she graduated from the U.S. Naval Academy. Cathleen was part of an illustrious club as her class was the second in the academy's history to admit women, which was met by resistance, harassment, and hatred. Attitudes toward women were far from welcoming, but she managed to hold her own and was up for the challenge.

She proved herself to be a driven and highly motivated cadet. On top of being very athletic, Cathleen received martial arts training during her time in the academy and was also a Russian scholar. This was vital as the tensions between the U.S. and the then Soviet Union were at an all-time high during the 1980s. Thomas was the second most improved Russian speaker in the entire academy during her time there.

Though only having served there for five years after graduating, Thomas did not dwell on it too much, even though she had wanted to make her father—a career Navy man—proud. Instead, she moved on to better things when her career as a stockbroker took off, and she ultimately realized that the Navy wasn't what she was meant to do. Besides, she wouldn't have met Rebecca Dowski had she not made the decision to move on. The pair formed an instant bond, and their friends mentioned that they would often drive to the Colonial Parkway to get some much-needed privacy. While there was not a great deal of outright homophobia in the conservative towns where they were, their relationship may not have been viewed with immediate acceptance by the majority of the locals.

David Knobling and Robin Edwards

After Thomas's and Dowski's bodies were found, the authorities were ready to chalk it up to a homophobic hate crime. However, things changed when another couple was shot dead in late September 1987, almost a year after the first two murders. This time it was 20-year-old David Knobling and 14-year-old Robin Edwards. Their bodies had been discovered in the Ragged Island Wildlife Refuge three days after their deaths on September 20, 1987. The refuge is located near the James Smith River in Smithfield, Virginia.

Knobling's prized black Ford Ranger pickup truck was found abandoned near the James River Bridge on September 20 by a county deputy. There were no signs of Knobling or Edwards; however, the keys were still in the ignition, and the door was open. Moreover, the windshield wipers had been turned on and were still working, as was the radio. Some clothing of both Knobling and Edwards was inside the truck, and while Knobling's wallet was there, Edwards's purse was not. This prompted a search led by Knobling's father to find the missing David and Robin. It was three days later that their bodies washed up on the beach in the refuge and were found by a jogger.

They had both been shot in the back of the head as if they were executed and then dumped in the river.

However, Knobling appeared to have tried to make a break for it, and thus, he was first shot in the shoulder, which most likely made him fall down, and then shot in the back of the head. Edwards was shot once in the back of the head. Much like the murders of Thomas and Dowski the previous year, besides the missing purse, there were no signs of robbery or sexual assault.

The refuge had a reputation as a popular party spot for teenagers, not to mention as a lover's lane, so it was surmised that Knobling and Edwards had ventured out there for some intimacy. This wasn't the first time for Knobling, as he had driven his Ford Ranger to Ragged Island several times from his house in Hampton, Virginia. According to Edwards's parents, Knobling had snuck into their house in Newport News, Virginia, to meet with Robin, following which they both snuck out and drove off. Even though Robin was only 14, a minor, Knobling was not the first older man she'd been with, as her parents admitted that she had been with a 21-year-old when she was only 11.

Reportedly, on the same night that they snuck away to the refuge, the two met at a movie screening in Newport News along with a group of friends. According to eyewitnesses, Knobling offered a lift to Edwards, her little brother, and their cousin and dropped them off at their home. Later that night, they both snuck out and headed to the refuge for the very last time.

Investigators found something peculiar this time: The driver's side window of Knobling's Ford Ranger was partially rolled down. This led them to surmise that as the victims were parked and about to get intimate, the killer may have approached them, posing as a law enforcement officer. Knobling and Edwards were then likely marched down at gunpoint to the marsh about a mile away, where they were finally executed.

Both Knobling and Edwards appeared to have troubling lives. David looked like he was going to have a promising future as he was working with his father in their landscaping business. Not only that, but he also actually had a steady longtime girlfriend who was expecting a child. However, David was clearly cheating on her with a 14-year-old girl. On the other hand, Robin Edwards had a history of mental illness, had previously run away from home on multiple occasions, and was known for her uncontrollable and reckless behavior. Although, she seemed to be showing signs of recovery after going into therapy, making tremendous progress before her untimely murder.

The Ragged Island Murders, as they came to be known, generated a great deal of notoriety. The nature of the victims' relationship and the scandal surrounding the lover's lane aspect of the murders was highly controversial, as was the fact that the site was only 20 miles away from the Colonial Parkway where the previous murders had occurred. This was enough for the media to catch wind and descend upon the refuge, which made the investigations even more difficult. Their constant movement around the area of the murders, coupled with rain, had made getting any more evidence nearly impossible.

While the media's constant pestering and speculation had tried to link any unsolved murders around that time with the Ragged Island Murders, it wasn't until about six-and-a-half months later that the subsequent murders in this grueling saga would take place.

Cassandra Lee Hailey and Richard Keith Call

The following year on April 10, 1988, a red Toyota Celica was found abandoned at the York River Overlook on the Colonial Parkway by a park ranger, who reported it at around 9 a.m. The car belonged to 20-year-old college student Richard 'Keith' Call, who was studying computer science at Christopher Newport University. According to witnesses, Call was last seen at a party in Newport News on the night of April 9, 1988, where he was on his first date with 18-year-old Cassandra Lee Hailey, a fellow student at the same college. But while Call's vehicle was found, neither Call nor Hailey has ever been located, despite many extensive searches. They are both presumed dead.

On the surface, this third incident appeared to be the work of the same person responsible for the earlier murders of Thomas, Dowski, Knobling, and Edwards. The key difference here is that no bodies were found along with or near the car. According to the authorities, it was believed that Hailey and Call both likely went skinny-dipping in the river and, unfortunately, drowned. Much like Knobling's truck, the keys were still on the driver's seat in Call's car, and a pair of glasses and a watch were left on the dashboard. A wallet with some cash and one set of men's clothing was present in the back seat, as well as some women's clothing. The woman's purse was on the floor, but her wallet was not inside.

Later, when the investigators from the previous scenes arrived, they realized that the water was freezing and thus made it unlikely that the missing victims had entered the water willingly. Because the officers on the scene went with the skinny-dipping theory, they had not initially reported the matter to the FBI. It wasn't until details started getting shared over police bulletins that the investigators from the previous crime scenes arrived. They were highly suspicious of the circumstances of this disappearance as the overlook was just three miles away from where Thomas and Dowski had been found murdered.

In a cruel twist, that same morning, Call's father was on his way to work via the parkway when he actually saw his son's car parked at the same location at 7 a.m. He stopped for a moment and called Keith's name, but there was no answer. He looked in through the windows, saw no one inside, and then simply drove on. According to eyewitnesses, Call and Hailey were at a party in Newport News and had left at around 2 a.m., which was the last anyone saw them. Hailey was a freshman and lived in York County, which is about five miles from where Call's car was found. Even though they went to the same college, it was Hailey's first date with Call, who lived in Gloucester, located across the river from where they disappeared.

Aided by a tide expert, the investigators believed that the bodies would take at least three days to resurface if they had been thrown into the York River. That is precisely what happened when a body did indeed surface; however, it turned out to be that of a middle-aged African American man. Richard Call was Caucasian. It was later discovered that the man had fallen into the river off of a boat some days before the discovery of Call's vehicle.

Even if this was all the work of the same individual, the victims seemed to have suffered very different fates. Thomas and Dowski had been strangled and nearly decapitated, Knobling and Edwards had been shot dead, while Call and Hailey had disappeared entirely without a trace. In all cases, the victims were in a relationship of some kind and looked to be getting intimate in a secluded area when the killer struck, likely having followed them. Call and Hailey only got to know each other for a few hours, and it would be the last thing they ever did before succumbing to their horrible fate.

If the authorities had been skeptical over whether or not these murders and disappearances were connected, it wouldn't take long for them to be absolutely certain when a fourth couple was found two years later.

Annamaria Phelps and Daniel Lauer

Right after the Labor Day weekend in 1989, a golden 1972 Chevrolet Nova was found abandoned at the New Kent rest stop on I-64 by a state trooper. Apparently, the vehicle was in the middle of the truck acceleration lane, which led onto the highway and almost caused a roadblock. The car belonged to 21-year-old Daniel Lauer, a resident of Amelia County near Richmond. On September 4, 1989, he left his home at about 11 p.m. with his brother's girlfriend, 18-year-old Annamaria Phelps. They were heading to Virginia Beach to meet with Lauer's brother and Phelps's boyfriend; Annamaria and Daniel's brother had been living in an apartment there, and she convinced Daniel to move out there with them.

While they were headed east, their car was found on the westbound side of the highway, roughly 30 miles away from the Colonial Parkway. When the vehicle was reported abandoned, the authorities sprang into action. Based on the previous incidents over the last few years, the detectives had set up sufficient victim criteria to be reported immediately, and the discovery of the Nova raised the appropriate red flags. Upon searching the vehicle, all of Lauer's belongings were found inside the car, as was a roach clip that belonged to Phelps. It was hanging out of the driver's side window and had long feathers attached to it. The only thing that appeared to be missing was Phelps's wallet, as it wasn't in her purse, and a blanket from the trunk. However, with no bodies around the scene, the investigators started a thorough search around the countryside as they hoped that the fresh disappearance would yield some immediate results.

But it wouldn't be until a month and a half later that some hunters discovered the skeletonized remains of both Lauer and Phelps on October 19, 1989. They were found along I-64 between Williamsburg and Richmond. Because of the hot and rainy weather prevalent in the weeks between their disappearance and discovery, the bodies had suffered advanced decomposition and had been picked apart by wild animals. Thus, it was impossible to determine the exact cause of death; however, some MRI scans showed that Phelps appeared to have been stabbed to death.

Aside from the similarities of the abandoned vehicles, this time, there were callbacks to the previous murders. Phelps appeared to have been stabbed and slashed just like Thomas and Dowski had been, while the bodies had been taken away from the vehicle just like Call and Hailey. This made the incidents appear connected, but the evidence available to the authorities was in bits and pieces.

After four years of terrorizing the residents of the nearby areas, there were no further reported incidents of abandoned vehicles and missing couples. The mysterious assailant mercilessly executed eight victims, and with no further incidents or evidence, the bizarre killings during the late 1980s became just that: a mystery.

The Investigation

Despite locating the abandoned vehicles in a relatively quick time frame, they were all discovered the day after the incidents took place, and the authorities never managed to get any credible leads or evidence. Considering that DNA investigation was still in its infancy, the few bits of circumstantial DNA evidence that were found did not point to any potential breakthroughs. Moreover, as the killings took place during the late nights and in secluded spots, and there were absolutely no witnesses who came forward.

The killer's motive has also remained unclear, as with the bodies found, there were no signs of any sexual molestation or struggles. In fact, in the cases of Knobling and Edwards, they appeared to have been taken willingly to their deaths. Even Thomas and Dowski seemed to have been subdued without any signs of a struggle, but they were placed in awkward positions. Thomas was found in the rear hatch of the Civic while Dowski was in the back seat with her foot stuck between the front seat and the door. In all cases, their vehicles appeared to be devoid of any signs of struggle. The keys were either in the ignition or carefully placed on a car seat.

As no sexual abuse was detected in the bodies that were found, it did not seem to be the likely reason they were targeted. Most of the wallets and purses were left in the car along with money, so theft could also be ruled out. There wasn't any connection between the victims, as they all lived in different towns and did not go to the same school. The only similarity they did have was that they were all Caucasian, in their teens or twenties, and that they were last seen together either on a date or at parties.

The only possible explanation as to why the killer went on such a rampage appeared to be just for the thrill of it. It is almost akin to the Monster of Florence, another prolific serial killer who operated in Italy during the 1960s, but the difference here is that the Colonial Parkway murders showed no signs of any kind of sexual gratification by the murderer. In their warped mind, they simply wanted to prey upon unsuspecting couples, catch them in the middle of the act, and end their lives.

The Suspects

Fred Atwell

Nicknamed the 'whistleblower,' Atwell was the deputy sheriff active during the investigation in 1986. However, he breathed new life into the case in 2009 when he revealed that about 84 graphic photographs of the Colonial Parkway Murders, including those of the bodies, had been provided to a security company for training purposes by the FBI. When he blew the lid off the photographs, the victims' families were outraged at what they considered to be the FBI's callous attitude towards their deceased loved ones. Though it is mere speculation at this point, the rest of Atwell's life was tainted with several run-ins with the law as a result of this incident. At one point, he was charged with committing a robbery of $100.

But that didn't stop Atwell from sounding out his opinion regarding the identity of the murderer, which ultimately put him on the FBI's radar as a suspect. His actions in 2009 earned him a heroic reputation among the families of the victims, who were very interested in what he had to say. Over time, though, Atwell's attitude became stranger, and he seemed to be purely interested in gaining publicity by inserting himself into the investigation, and he also started making outlandish claims. None of the families believe that Atwell was responsible in any way, and they considered him to be the FBI's scapegoat for embarrassing them. Regardless, Atwell never fully divulged any secrets he supposedly had right up to his death in 2018.

A Disturbed Vietnam Veteran

In 1990, while the media attention was still focused on the Colonial Parkway Murders, the authorities had instituted a tip line that began being flooded with calls. This took place after the FBI held a press conference in Norfolk along with the state police, and sure enough, leads were coming in from all over. On one such phone call, a hospital nurse phoned in, stating that one of her patients outright claimed that he "killed those kids." This incident took place in September 1987, and by those kids, he was referring to David Knobling and Robin Edwards. This was a sea of change, especially considering that up until that point, clues had been few and far between.

But the nurse had only remembered this after watching a documentary about the murders. According to her description, the man was a Vietnam veteran who was suffering from blackouts. He had several periods which were unaccounted for, and he could not remember anything from those times. He had come into the hospital visibly disturbed and upset just a few days after the bodies of Knobling and Edwards were found.

Once the FBI questioned the suspect, they found that while he had the capacity to kill someone, he lacked the organizational and planning skills that were the hallmark of these killings. Moreover, there was no physical evidence that connected this veteran to the crimes. The man was, by all accounts, deeply emotionally disturbed due to a rough childhood, his horrifying experience in the war, and his dismal employment record. Therefore, he was ruled out as a suspect in the Colonial Parkway Murders.

The United Front

While the Colonial Parkway Murders remain an open case, they are also one of many that are under investigation by the FBI. However, sadly there seems to be no tangible headway toward solving these killings. Nevertheless, the families of the victims and the surviving siblings are wholly committed and determined to find the killer after all these years. They have placed their faith in the tremendous developments in forensic science and DNA testing, which was still in its early stages in the late 1980s. They believe that somehow forensic genealogy will be able to unearth the truth that has evaded them for nearly 40 years.

The families of the eight victims have remained in touch since the late 1980s, brought together by their shared grief and the ever-growing frustration over the lack of progress by the authorities, the FBI in particular. It began with the parents of the victims, but after all this time, the siblings are carrying the baton forward as they try to unearth the truth behind the gruesome murders. Bill Thomas, brother of Cathleen Thomas, has been instrumental in this movement by managing a social media page and a podcast to ensure awareness among the public of these crimes. Thomas and members of the other families continue to pursue any leads they receive and follow up with investigators. They also provide interviews to media, including newspapers, T.V. channels, and the internet, on a recurring basis to ensure that the events of the Colonial Parkway are never forgotten.

2

THE OAKLAND COUNTY CHILD KILLER

If you've ever lived in a small town, then you understand how it can be rare to cross the path of a stranger. Everyone knows everyone else in these tight-knit communities, which can simultaneously be a blessing and a curse. For millennia, children have been given more freedom to explore their surroundings than their modern-day counterparts, but eventually, newspapers and televised newscasts would do their best to spread pertinent information to the public. Still, it really wasn't until the birth of the internet that being an over-protective parent started to become more and more commonplace. If only technology had advanced more rapidly, the number of lives saved would be staggering.

Oakland County, Michigan, used to be the kind of place where parents could let their children play outside carefree, but that all started to change in the 1970s when an evil presence shattered their innocence. Four towns where four young children, both boys, and girls, were ripped from their lives with family and friends and killed by a highly depraved individual who came to be known as the Oakland County Child Killer.

The Victims

Mark Stebbins

On February 15, 1976, 12-year-old Mark Stebbins headed out from the American Legion Hall at 1:30 in the afternoon and was on his way home. Before he left, he contacted his mother over the phone to let her know he was coming. But when he hadn't turned up by 11 o'clock at night, his mother reported him missing to the Ferndale Police Department. Four days later, a businessman was heading toward a drug store at New Orleans Mall at around 11:45 a.m. As he was heading to the parking lot, he noticed something in the corner that he first mistook for a mannequin. It wasn't till he got closer that he recoiled in horror at seeing it was not a mannequin dressed in a jacket and jeans, but actually the dead body of a young boy.

The authorities were able to identify the body as that of the missing Mark Stebbins. But this was no accident, as they uncovered the full extent of the horrors inflicted on the 12-year-old. Stebbins had been smothered and asphyxiated to death, and his neck, wrists, and ankles had been bound with rope, made apparent by visible rope burns. Even more chilling, Mark appeared to have been sexually assaulted, and his body had either been bathed after he was killed, or he was forced to bathe before being murdered. Thus any forensic evidence, including DNA samples, fingerprints, and so on, was lost.

Stebbins had been living with his mother in Ferndale, Michigan, after his parents had divorced. He was in 7th grade at the Lincoln Junior High School and came from a Roman Catholic family. While he was described as a quiet and good student, Stebbins usually kept to himself and was by all accounts a loner.

Jill Robinson

Nearly a year after Stebbins was murdered, another child went missing in a town nearby. Just over 2 miles away from Ferndale, the city of Royal Oak, Michigan, was stunned when another 12-year-old, Jill Robinson, went missing on the evening of December 22, 1976. Much like Stebbins, Robinson's parents had also been divorced, and she was staying with her mother in Royal

Oak. The eldest of three daughters, Jill Robinson, had an argument with her mother that evening over, of all things, cookies. She had apparently been asked to help with the cooking, but when she refused, she had a heated argument with her mother, Karol.

That was when Karol laid down the law and told her to leave the house until she became a part of the family. Obviously incensed, Jill packed up her clothes into a plaid denim bag, changed into an orange winter coat, a pair of blue jeans, a shirt, and a blue and yellow knit cap, and then took off on her bike. A family friend claimed to have spotted her at a hobby shop on Woodward Avenue the same evening, and two witnesses said they had seen her on Maple Road at the Donut Depot between 6 and 7 a.m. on December 23, 1976.

That was the last anyone had seen Jill Robertson alive. The night that she disappeared, her father, Thomas, reported her missing at 11:30 p.m. She wouldn't be seen again till after Christmas Day when her body was discovered on the I-75 near Troy, Michigan, roughly eight miles away from Royal Oak. The cause of death was a shotgun wound to the head at close range, but she had been brought to that location and then killed. This was evidenced by the ring of dried blood around her head where she had been left. She was fully clothed, and surprisingly, there were no signs of sexual abuse. Upon further examination, it appeared that Robinson had been kept in captivity and provided food and drink till she was killed, but there were no signs of rope burns or that she had been tied up. And in a chilling similarity to Stebbins' murder, Robinson appeared to have been bathed before being killed, likely to wash away any forensic evidence.

There are several glaring similarities between Stebbins and Robinson. Aside from each being 12 years old, both kids' parents were divorced, and they were living with their mothers. They also came from Roman Catholic families, and Robinson was also described as an intelligent and capable student but a loner, just like Stebbins. The only differences are the method of execution and the fact that Robinson had not been sexually abused, unlike Stebbins.

Kristine Mihelich

The murderer did not look like he was going to stop any time soon, as only ten days later, another child went missing in Michigan. This time it was 10-year-old Kristine Mihelich, a resident of Berkley, Michigan, which is only two and a half miles away from Royal Oaks and four and a half miles away from Ferndale. Much like Stebbins and Robinson, Mihelich was also living with her mother after her divorce. She was regarded as a quiet and introverted student who kept to herself. As a fifth-grader at Pattengill Elementary School, her teachers reported her as an average student.

Shortly after Mihelich's disappearance, the authorities formed a task force of thirty-five officers from nine different departments to track down the missing child. This was regarded to be the most substantial effort ever seen in Oakland County.

To say that Kristine's disappearance caused a panic is a colossal understatement. Right after she vanished, another student went missing from the same school but was found shortly thereafter. Nevertheless, the residents were on edge and had become highly protective. After the discovery of Robinson's body only days before, parents were no longer risking their children's safety. For starters, they had begun picking up their kids from school instead of letting them walk home.

Nearly 20 days after she disappeared, a body was found frozen in a snowbank in Franklin Village by a mail carrier on January 21, 1977. The mail carrier was frightened to see a hand sticking out of the snowbank and immediately alerted the authorities. But once the body was removed from the snowbank, there was no doubt that it belonged to Kristine Mihelich. Because of its frozen state, it took a full day before an autopsy could be performed. Once it was checked, they determined that Mihelich had been suffocated to death; however, there were no signs of sexual assault. She was also fully clothed and wearing the same outfit she had been in when she was last seen.

Despite several key similarities, there was still no clear evidence linking any of the three victims.

Timothy King

The killer waited nearly three months after Mihelich's disappearance before striking again. This time he went after 11-year-old Timothy King, who had left his home in Birmingham, Michigan, to go to a corner store on the evening of March 16, 1977. He had about 30 cents with him and was looking to get some candy. Timothy was last seen by the store clerk who sold him candy and saw him leave through the back door that led into a dark parking lot. This was around 8:30 p.m., after which he was not seen alive again. The trip from the store to his house was roughly three blocks, and it was one that King used to take on a regular basis. He also had his skateboard and football with him when he left home.

Unlike the previous three victims, Timothy King was different. His parents were not divorced though he did come from a Roman Catholic background. According to those who knew him, King was actually very outgoing, friendly, and well-liked. However, he still did not talk to strangers and would generally run away if he ever encountered someone he didn't know. Timothy was also athletic and talented as he played basketball and was in a school play. At the time he disappeared, his parents were having dinner at a nearby restaurant. Timothy had borrowed money for candy from his older sister Catherine while his older brothers were out babysitting and rehearsing for a school project. Nevertheless, Catherine also went out for the night but remembered to leave the front door unlocked so that Timothy could back get inside.

When Timothy's parents returned home after 9 o'clock that night, they were troubled to see that he wasn't at home and that the door was open. Already tense from the previous abductions and murders that had taken place in the county, King's parents immediately mobilized friends and neighbors to search for him. Tensions reached an all-time high when over 100 Oakland County officers, volunteers, investigators, and even the county helicopter were out combing through the area trying to find any sign of Timothy King. They conducted door-to-door searches and questioned all of King's classmates and neighbors.

Timothy's parents also made a plea to the kidnapper on television, stating they wanted him back and that they would take him to get his favorite meal at Kentucky Fried Chicken.

Seven days later, King's body was found about 20 miles away from Birmingham in Livonia, Michigan, in a ditch near the 8 Mile Road on March 23, 1977. This is the farthest that any of the victims had been left from their hometowns. The area was a dirt road not that far from a busy intersection, which is where a motorist came upon King's body and alerted the authorities. King was clad in the same clothes he had been wearing when he left home, and his skateboard was also dumped nearby. According to the autopsy, King was well taken care of during his captivity. In a cruel twist, it seemed the killer, and possibly Timothy himself, watched Mr. and Mrs. King on the news because prior to his death Timothy was given his favorite meal of Kentucky Fried Chicken. Before killing him, the murderer also ensured that King was bathed and adequately groomed. He had also been suffocated to death and, for the first time since Stebbins, and to everyone's horror, had also been sexually assaulted.

Only one glimmer of hope emerged after this incident as the authorities got their first-ever description of a suspect claimed to have been seen with King before the abduction. Shortly after the disappearance, a woman informed the officers that she had seen a boy she believed to be King in the parking lot talking to a man. According to her description, the man was between the ages of 25 and 35, Caucasian, with dark brown shaggy hair and mutton chop sideburns. He also had a husky build and was seen driving a dark blue AMC Gremlin with white stripes on the side.

Sensing that the task force was beginning to get hot on his tail, the activities of the Oakland County Child Killer came to an abrupt end.

The Investigation

By Oakland County's standards, the investigation into the disappearances and murders of the four children was the most concentrated and exhaustive. However, they had their work cut out for them, considering that there were near to no witnesses to the actual abductions. All of the witnesses who had seen the victims claimed that they seemed fine and going about their day as usual. Once the authorities started seeking help, several tips started rolling in, which required extensive man-hours to follow up and make sure they were valid or otherwise.

There were several different projects that the special task force carried out in 1977, aiming to apprehend the Oakland County Child Killer once and for all. These include Operation Observation which used a composite sketch of the suspect as described by the witness in King's abduction, and Operation Victimization, which collated data regarding all the reported incidents of sexual offenses committed in the county in order to follow up on those leads to find a credible match. Other projects included Operations Lure, Family Background, Unsolved Homicides-Nationwide and Worldwide, Burial Ritual, and Back-Up and Support.

Aside from the task force's activities, the people of the communities also started coming together to unearth clues regarding the tragedies that befell these children. During King's disappearance, his father, Barry King, appealed publicly on local TV channels in the hopes that the kidnappers would listen and return their son to them unharmed. He also urged the authorities and the Birmingham Police Department, in particular, to leave no stone unturned and treat the search for Timothy King as if they were searching for their own children. His quest to find the identity of his son's killer continues to this date.

The Suspects

From the profile the investigators were able to create after collecting all possible leads stemming from the four murders, the killer appeared to be highly intelligent, sophisticated, and appear trustworthy enough for children to be able to like upon instinct. With three of the bodies not showing signs of struggle, it is very likely that the children were able to trust the killer either because of their friendly quality or perhaps because they were local and part of the community.

What is known is that the killer is male and was between 20 to 30 years old at the time, Caucasian, well-educated, and highly intelligent. He also appeared to have homosexual tendencies as he had sexually assaulted two boys but did not do so with the girls. He also had a knack for cleanliness. He bathed the victims before killing them either because of mental compulsion or because it was deliberate as he wanted to wash away any forensic evidence. Furthermore, the killer appeared to have some sort of affinity for children as he ensured they were looked after and well-fed while in captivity. Frighteningly, he also had a premises where he could keep the children hidden for as long as 19 days in the case of Mihelich. Finally, the killer wanted his victims to be found, though it is not clear if it is because he wanted to give closure to the families or because he wanted to instill fear in the community.

Christopher Busch

A suspect believed to be the Oakland County Child Killer by many authorities, as well as Timothy King's family, was convicted pedophile Christopher Busch. A resident of Bloomfield Hills, Michigan, the 26-year-old Busch seemed a likely suspect after the authorities were pointed in his direction by 27-year-old Gregory

Greene in 1977. Greene himself had been arrested on charges of child sexual assault, which is when he directed the police to Busch, claiming that Christopher had killed Stebbins. However, investigators revealed that he had been in police custody while the murders were being investigated. It was during this incarceration that Busch admitted he was a pedophile, and he had also passed a polygraph test where he claimed that he did not kill any of the children in the Oakland County Child Killer murders. Even though the investigators wanted to keep him incarcerated, Busch made a plea deal and was released. Shortly after, he committed suicide in 1978.

But the King family was not convinced. When the authorities photographed the scene of Busch's suicide, the photographs showed specific evidence that could tie him to the Oakland County Child Killer. In one photo, there was a drawing on Busch's wall which showed a boy being tortured who resembled the first victim, Mark Stebbins. Another showed a shotgun shell, and another had some ropes with blood on them. These items could easily be tied back to the murders of Stebbins and Robinson. As if that weren't enough, Busch owned a blue Chevrolet Vega, which looked similar to the AMC Gremlin that had been spotted in King's abduction.

But despite the family's best efforts, the shotgun shell caliber was not the same that was used in Robinson's murder. Moreover, the forensic scientist who conducted the analysis on the ropes shown in the photographs claimed that there actually wasn't any blood on them, as he would have sent it to the evidence unit if there had been. By 2012, however, DNA conclusively proved that there was no link between Busch and any of the physical evidence collected by investigators in the Oakland County Child Killer murders.

As for Greene, he had also passed a polygraph test at around the same time as Busch. He was then convicted of assaulting young boys and sentenced to life in prison.

James Vincent Gunnels

The closest suspect to have emerged from the investigation was James Vincent Gunnels when his DNA was found to be a mitochondrial DNA match—belonging to the suspect or a male relative on the suspect's mother's side—to a hair that had been found on Kristine Mihelich's body. Moreover, he had also failed a lie detector test. However, Gunnels maintained that he was not responsible for any of the killings and claimed that he was being set up by the state police. Furthermore, he claimed that at the time, he was a part of an organized ring led by Christopher Busch and that he had himself been sexually assaulted by Busch. He was 16 at the time.

He also claimed to be sympathetic to the victim's families and even tried reaching out to them for a face-to-face meeting, starting with the family of Timothy King. Intent on seeking justice for Timothy, Barry King and Chris King, Timothy's brother, did, in fact, meet with Gunnels, who told them about Busch, but that led nowhere. Nevertheless, Gunnels maintains his innocence in the matter of the Oakland County Child Killer murders despite being the first-ever confirmed DNA match with the physical evidence collected at the scene of Mihelich's murder.

But even with the DNA match, there is no other solid evidence that can tie Gunnels to the murders. With a history of property-related crimes, the theory by the investigators is that Gunnels was part of a ring of sexual predators, and his primary role was to lure unsuspecting children resulting in their abduction. While they do not believe that Gunnels was the Oakland County Child Killer, his own admission as an accessory to the crime is damning. Gunnels was actually under police custody until April 2011, when he was released and has since been living in Kalamazoo in a halfway house.

The Aftermath

It should come as no surprise that the King family was not at all happy when they discovered the plea deal of Christopher Busch. They firmly believed that Busch was the one responsible, considering all the evidence that had been uncovered at the scene of his suicide; evidence that seems to have been ignored and now vanished. Even after Barry King's death in 2020, the rest of the King family will not rest until they find out who exactly was responsible for the killings all those years ago.

3

THE DISAPPEARED OF ISÈRE

Serial killers are certainly callous, but the one thing that sets them apart from everyone else is their total lack of empathy. Reasonable people recognize that human suffering need not be suffered alone, and it helps when there is someone there to look out for them in their time of need. But what if the very people chosen to be custodians of the citizens' lives show a completely brazen and indifferent attitude towards the plight of the innocent? What if the same people who protect the populace from all threats and see that justice is done drag their feet in dispensing it? What if they simply just don't care?

This was the case for the French authorities in the department of Isère, where 12 children were abducted from right outside of their own homes between 1983 and 1996. Some children were found murdered, and some were never to be seen or heard from again.

This is the story of "Les disparus de l'Isère" (The Disappeared of the Isère).

The Victims

The Disappeared of Isère were all children between the ages of 5 and 15 and mostly belonged to immigrant families that had been living in public housing facilities in the area. Most of these disappearances occurred during the afternoon while the children were near their homes and within a radius of roughly 44 miles between the localities of Lyon and Grenoble. As stated, several of these children have never been recovered and are presumed dead, but some were found murdered, with strangulation being the chief cause of death. Only one child was found alive. Moreover, the bodies that were found also had clear signs of sexual assault.

To date, a total of 12 children have been considered among Les disparus de l'Isère, and they all went missing during an extended period from 1980 to 1996. That is seventeen years of fear and uncertainty that the victims' families have endured. Still, their disdain is also aimed at the efforts of the different authorities in charge of the investigations. With the disappearances occurring somewhat regularly over almost two decades, one would assume a large task force was on the hunt for whoever was responsible. However, over the years, the cases themselves have often been dismissed, abandoned, or even misplaced altogether. Needless to say, this has both shocked and angered the victims' families, who have regularly voiced the need for a single investigating judge to take over all the cases of the missing and murdered children. But their demands, so far, have fallen on deaf ears.

Philippe Pignot

The first victim to disappear, or at least potentially considered among Les disparus de l'Isère, is Philippe Pignot. He vanished on May 25, 1980, from La Morte-sur-Isère when he was just 13 years old. He has never been seen or heard from again. The reason why Pignot has not been permanently included in the list of The Disappeared is because of a lack of evidence to connect him with the others. Hence, his case has been separated but needs to be mentioned here.

Ludovic Janvier

Officially starting the list off is six-year-old Ludovic Janvier, who vanished on March 17, 1983, near Saint-Martin-d'Hères, located in the Grenoble suburbs. According to witnesses, Janvier had left his house and gone shopping with his brothers when they were approached by a man. The man was asking for help to find his dog when he abducted Janvier. Like Phillipe Pignot, Janvier has also never been found.

Grégory Dubrulle

A few months after Janvier's disappearance, seven-year-old Grégory Dubrulle was found in a garbage dump site in Pommiers-la-Placette. He had gone missing just a day before, on July 9, 1983, when he was seen being forced into a white Mercedes. He had been violently hit on the head, thus sustaining injuries, but he was thankfully found alive and made a full recovery. Due to the nature of his injuries, however, he was unable to provide details about what had happened to him.

Unidentified Remains

It wouldn't be until around two years later when the skeletonized remains of an unidentified child were found in the Vercors Caves on May 23, 1985. No connection could be made between this discovery and the other victims, despite the fact that the body belonged to a child around the same age as Janvier. Based on examinations, the cause of death was a shattered skull. It was likely that before being found, the body had been dumped in the caves several months, if not years prior, which made the task of recovering any helpful forensic evidence next to impossible.

Anissa Ouadi

Five-year-old Anissa Ouadi disappeared on June 25, 1985, from Grenoble. She was apparently playing football near her housing estate at around 5:30 p.m. when she vanished. Her body was found in the Beauvoir Dam in Isère on July 9, 1985, 13 days after her disappearance. According to the autopsy, she appeared to have been strangled and then drowned.

Charazed Bendouiou

Two years later, 10-year-old Charazed Bendouiou went missing from Bourgoin-Jallieu on July 8, 1987. She had asked her mother for permission to play football at around 1:00 p.m. outside their housing estate in the Champ-Fleuri district but instead was last seen in her building's basement emptying the trash. No further clues or witness statements were reported.

Nathalie Boyer

A year later, 15-year-old Nathalie Boyer vanished from Villefontaine on August 2, 1988, while she was out for a walk. Two days later, she was found dead by a railway worker near the train tracks in Saint-Quentin-Fallavier on August 4, 1988. The cause of death was a slit throat.

Fabrice Ladoux

By now, a pattern seemed to be emerging as the children were being picked off each year during the summer months. But that would change when just five months later, 12-year-old Fabrice Ladoux was abducted in Grenoble on January 13, 1989. He was on the path from his school to his house when he disappeared. His body was found three days later in the Chartreuse Mountains, and the cause of death appeared to be a violent head wound similar to Grégory Dubrulle. But to the disgust and horror of the authorities, Ladoux seemed to have been sexually assaulted before his murder.

Rachid Bouzian

There had been three disappearances, with three bodies found in a row and one that had been sexually assaulted. This pattern continued over a year later when eight-year-old Rachid Bouzian was the next one to vanish from his building in Échirolles on August 3, 1990, while he was playing outside at around 7:30 p.m. Two days later, his body was found wrapped inside a blanket in an underground garage located about 200 yards from his house. Bouzian had been sexually assaulted as well.

On August 23, 1990, a suspect was arrested in connection to the crime for the first time. This man—Karim Katefi—was arrested for his part in the abduction, but he maintains that his brother had instigated the crime. However, this brother had fled the country, and thus the suspect was found guilty of both the abduction and murder. Katefi was subsequently sentenced to life in prison, where he eventually died.

Sarah Siad

Unfortunately, that was not the end of the misery in Isère. A year later, six-year-old Sarah Siad vanished from a playground in Voreppe near her housing estate of Bourg-Vieux on April 15, 1991, between 6:00 p.m. and 7:00 p.m. This meant that the killer, or at least an associate of the man in prison, was still out there, and he continued with the terrifying crimes. Siad was found dead the next day, on April 16, 1991, in a wooded area roughly 300 yards from her home. The cause of death was strangulation, but she had also been sexually assaulted. Only this time, the investigators were able to collect some trace DNA evidence, including some semen samples from Siad's blouse and some thumbprints from her body. While the state of DNA analysis was unable to yield any credible results, the evidence was sealed for future investigative purposes.

Léo Balley

The next five years had the residents of Isère holding their breaths. The summer of 1992 passed with relative calm, then the next, and the next, and the next, and it seemed as if the children of Isère were safe at last. But on July 19, 1996, another child named Léo Balley vanished while on a hike with his father on the Massif du Taillefer. While his father was setting up the tent, the six-year-old Balley disappeared, and a Citroën BX was seen in the area. Though it was discovered that the car was registered in the Bouches-du-Rhône, the lead did not pan out, and Balley was never found, bringing a return to the older pattern of bodies that were never located.

Saïda Berch

That same year, ten-year-old Saïda Berch vanished from Voreppe while she was returning home from the local gymnasium on November 24, 1996, at around 4:30 p.m. The gymnasium was located roughly 100 yards away from her house. This time, however, Berch's body was found near a canal in Voreppe nearly half a mile away from her home two days later, on November 26, 1996. The cause of death also appeared to be strangulation, and her own sweatshirt was used to choke the life out of her.

The Investigation

Despite the arrest and sentencing of the single suspect responsible for the murder of Rachid Bouzian in 1990, the other killings were never solved, largely because the investigators and the prosecutors who took over the successive cases could not arrive at the conclusion that this was the work of a serial killer. While there were similarities in the head wounds inflicted on Grégory Dubrulle and Fabrice Ladoux, there was still no concrete evidence available to form a connection.

Nevertheless, the victims' families remained persistent and were successful in reopening certain case files in March 2008. A new unit called the Mineurs 38 unit—literally translated as Minors 38—started to reexamine the cases. The '38' in Minors 38 refers to the Isère French departmental code, and the unit consists of several investigators and criminal analysts. This provided renewed hope to the family members of the victims.

The Conviction

On July 23, 2013, a 37-year-old man named Georges Pouille from Isère was arrested and charged for the murder and attempted rape of Sarah Siad in 1991 and for the murder of Saïda Berch in 1996. The events that led to Pouille's arrest are a testament to the power of forensic science and DNA investigation. Pouille had once been arrested for a traffic offense in December 2005 when he was caught driving under the influence of narcotics and not possessing valid documentation. As he was processed for this charge, his fingerprints had been uploaded to the French national automated database of genetic fingerprints (FNAEG).

Their sealed evidence was ordered to be reexamined by the investigating judge in March 2013, and the advances in forensic sciences enabled the investigators to match the thumbprints found on Siad's body with those of Pouille. The same fingerprints were found to be a match for the evidence collected at the sites where Siad and Berch's bodies were located. By the time Pouille was arrested—around two decades after Siad's murder—he was happily married and living in Isère with a child of his own. However, his health had deteriorated as he suffered muscle degeneration due to Steinert's disease. Since then, he has been retired, walks with a limp and is not considered violent or dangerous.

Initially, Pouille completely denied having anything to do with either Siad or Berch, claiming that he had never seen them and even swore on the life of his son, who was around three years old. Upon further questioning, Pouille kept making changes to his claims and later stated that he had actually come upon Siad as two other men were dumping her body.

According to Pouille, these men fled upon seeing him, and he went to check Siad for a pulse. When he did not find any, he claims to have been overcome by "a stroke of madness" or come under the influence of "the devil." His recollection of what happened next is vague, but he did recall masturbating over the dead body, which would explain the semen sample. In the case of Berch, Pouille stated that she had come to him to borrow his bicycle. Even after complying, Berch repeatedly asked him if she could keep the bike, which infuriated him, and thus he hit her on the head. He then strangled her with her own sweatshirt and dumped her near the canal. Pouille again feigned memory lapses but claimed he believed that Berch's demise was simply an accident.

According to the prosecution, Pouille was also familiar with the family members of Siad and Berch as he happened to know their brothers. He had even stayed in touch with them when he entrusted the care of his son to one of the victims' mothers, who happened to be a nurse.

While Pouille has yet to be tried and the other victims have received no justice, sadly, the media and the authorities consider this chapter in the grisly saga of The Disappeared of the Isère closed.

The Aftermath

With only the families of Siad and Berch getting the closure they had been waiting 20 years for, there are still several families whose children have not gotten justice. Moreover, the families have been distraught and enraged at the attitude of the authorities toward the investigation from the very start.

For instance, in the case of Charazed Bendouiou, the police didn't even meet with her parents until after the first day she went missing. As they were from North Africa and did not speak French, the police had a difficult time with Charazed's sister Ferouz Bendouiou translating for them. In interviews, she recalled that her family had not been taken seriously even after her father went to the station every day to find out the progress of the investigation. In fact, she alleged that the police were actually indifferent to them due to racial prejudice.

Over a decade later, Ferouz Bendouiou was shocked when she heard on a radio program that the file on The Disappeared of the Isère was about to be closed without any notice to the families. Even the toll-free number that was provided by the authorities had been switched off weeks prior.

In the case of Ludovic Janvier, the authorities claimed that they had received a call a month after his disappearance from someone saying that Janvier had been adopted by a childless couple and was happy. When Janvier's family demanded that the authorities provide them with an affidavit of the same, they were informed that the file had disappeared. Later on, expert lawyers were brought in and wanted access to the files, at which point Janvier's file, which had earlier vanished, miraculously reappeared. To the shock of the family, the file had practically nothing in it as it was just under three-quarters of an inch thick.

As if that weren't enough, the skeletonized remains of the unidentified child—who happened to be the same age as Janvier—were said to be destroyed by order of the authorities. When this news was brought to light, an inquiry was instituted, after which the authorities claimed that the remains had not been destroyed but were misplaced, never to be found again.

This careless attitude on the part of the authorities and even the media of the time resulted in at least one child killer remaining free to this day.

4

THE B1 BUTCHER

Cruelty can be found everywhere, no matter what part of the world you are in. And from 2005 to 2007, several families experienced up close and personal how violence can get out of hand, as the B1 Butcher took the lives of five young women in Namibia and dumped their remains along Namibia's National Road, B1. Known also as the "Khomas Ripper" based on the region where the remains were found, the killer showed the otherwise unassuming population of Namibia what cruelty could truly be.

The Victims

The B1 Butcher has been credited with the killings of five women, both young and middle-aged, and all native Namibians. Three of these victims were known sex workers who were active in the downtown area of Ausspannplatz in the Namibian capital. The other two victims could not be identified, though all of the victims showed signs of their bodies being in cold storage before they were discovered, suggesting a link between them.

The cause of death varied, including strangulation and blunt-force trauma to the head. Furthermore, the three victims who were identified were fluent in either Afrikaans or Damara, or both. Some of the victims also knew each other as they frequented the same areas to solicit clients interested in sexual favors.

Melanie Janse

On August 20, 2005, Melanie Janse was found dead on a bypass road in Windhoek. She was 22 years old, and her body was completely naked when it was discovered at the Van Eck Power Station. There were signs of blunt-force trauma to the chest and abdomen; however, the cause of death appeared to be strangulation. A former sex worker who knew Janse claimed that Melanie was also a sex worker, along with another victim who would be found later: Sanna Helena ǁGaroës. This unidentified sex worker claimed that both she and Janse solicited clients together.

Juanita Mabula

A month after Janse's body was found, another resident of Windhoek named Juanita Mabula went missing and was found dead near the Western Bypass. She had been killed and decapitated, and the body was discovered on September 25, 2005, along the bypass near the Windhoek Turf Club and Windhoek Country Club. Her head, on the other hand, was found between Rehoboth and Windhoek next to a culvert, or drain tunnel, on the B1 a month later, on October 24, 2005. The examination revealed that Mabula had been killed by blunt-force trauma to the back of the head. The authorities also believed that she was a commercial sex worker, but her family has denied this claim.

Sanna Helena ǁ Garoës

The dismembered body parts of 36-year-old Sanna Helena ǁGaroës were found over the course of four weeks at different locations on the main roads of Windhoek. Born on December 14, 1970, in Kalkrand, her last known whereabouts were in the city center at a restaurant called Zum Wirt on Independence Avenue at around 11 p.m. on June 13, 2007. She would not be seen again until three and a half days later, on June 17, 2007, when a human torso was found in a dumpster outside Windhoek. The torso had been dissected into two halves and dumped near the B1, 25 miles away from the city within the jurisdiction of Otjozondjupa and Okahandja.

At the time, the police could not be certain that the torso belonged to ǁGaroës. But three days later, more body parts would emerge as two human thighs were found in a different dumpster 15 miles away from Rehoboth near the B1. These thighs, just like the torso before, were cold to the touch, which led to the speculation that the body parts had been kept in cold storage. The location of this discovery was barely 10 miles away from where Juanita Mabula's body had been unearthed only a couple of years prior.

When the thighs were shown to ǁGaroës mother, Lena Engelbrecht, she identified a previous bullet wound as belonging to her daughter. But it wouldn't be officially confirmed until the fourth week after she went missing that the body parts belonged to Sanna. That's when a cluster of additional limbs was found on July 11, 2007, including a head, the lower legs, and feet—each of which had three missing toes. Though her hands remain missing, these body parts were discovered near the B6/Trans-Kalahari road, around 20 miles away from Windhoek, heading to the Kutako International Airport. A group of farmhands who were working nearby on repairing a fence came upon this gruesome discovery.

According to another former sex worker who claimed to know both ǁGaroës and Juanita Mabula, ǁGaroës was also a sex worker who used to solicit clients in the areas of Independence Avenue and Ausspannplatz with the Zum Wirt Bar and Restaurant the spot she frequented most. She also believed that the killer could have been a regular customer of ǁGaroës' or of sex workers in general. She also claimed to have seen Sanna about a week before her disappearance.

The investigators believe that the manner of dissection of both ǁGaroës and Mabula's bodies appeared to be the work of the same killer. Furthermore, ǁGaroës remains weren't the only ones that were found in those dumpsters between Okahandja and Rehoboth along the B1. Other parts that belonged to a different woman were also placed in those dumpsters and wrapped in garbage bags. This was similar to two other unsolved murders which had taken place since 2005 and are also believed to be the work of the B1 Butcher.

Other Related Incidents

As no concrete headway has been made to uncover the identity of the B1 Butcher, there is every likelihood that the killings that seemed to stop in 2007 could happen again. Moreover, considering the victims so far were known sex workers, the chances of any more being reported missing remain slim, considering police and public attitudes to these workers in general.

A few months after ǁGaroës remains were identified, a severed human head was found in Grootfontein on September 17, 2007, which the police claimed belonged to a woman named Jacoba Olivier. Ten days later, on

September 27, the police found more body parts that they believed were also Olivier's.

Jacoba Olivier was reported missing by her mother in 2003, and when the remains were discovered in 2007, a photograph of the head was published in newspapers and broadcast on news channels. In response to this, a woman approached the police and claimed that the skull belonged to Olivier. This was later confirmed when she saw it in the mortuary, and she also called Olivier's mother at her residence in Mariental to confirm this. With both mother and aunt seeing the head separately and having agreed that it belonged to Jacoba Olivier, the authorities were confident that the remains belonged to Jacoba and released a picture of her to solicit any information about her whereabouts after she disappeared in 2003.

But the story took an embarrassing turn for the police when it emerged only a month later that not only did the parts not belong to Jacoba Olivier but that she was perfectly alive and well and living in Outjo. She had been hospitalized in October 2007 and was visited by someone who showed her her own picture announcing her death in the newspaper. At this, she informed the police and let them know that she was indeed still alive and had been living in Outjo since 2003, after willingly leaving home.

There was a similar scare in 2010 when a human head and arm were discovered in Rehoboth. However, no connection could be made to the previous victims of the B1 Butcher. These more recent discoveries were made on a farm, not on highways such as the B1. Also, the B1 Butcher had held the dissected body parts in cold storage prior to dumping them, but these parts were found burnt.

The Suspects

Heinz Knierim

The first suspect to emerge was Heinz Knierim, a German national accused and arrested in August 2007 for the rape and attempted murder by strangulation of a 29-year-old unnamed Namibian woman near Windhoek. This pattern of sexual abuse and attempted strangulation of the victim matched with the modus operandi of the B1 Butcher; however, Knierim denied all such allegations. With no evidence tying Knierim to any of the B1 Butcher victims, he was acquitted in February 2010 of the charges. Knierim then proceeded to sue the Namibian government for wrongfully accusing him of being the B1 Butcher.

Hans Husselmann

Another suspect was 40-year-old Hans Husselmann, who was circumstantially tied to the B1 Butcher killings. The DNA of Sanna Helena ǁGaroës was found in Husselmann's house in Rehoboth, and his DNA was discovered on a letter received by the police, which contained information regarding the murder of Juanita Mabula. Though the DNA evidence was under investigation, it did not prove to be conclusive in pointing the fingers at Husselmann.

Husselmann was released from prison on parole on February 6, 2004. He had been serving a life sentence awarded to him in June 1989 for committing two murders and served 14 years and eight months. Aside from the DNA evidence collected, Mabula's body was found in September 2005, while Husselmann was a free man.

Unfortunately, the trail led nowhere as, after being implicated in the B1 Butcher murders, Hans Husselmann committed suicide by hanging at the age of 40 on June 19, 2008. In his suicide note, he declared that his choice to end his life was a matter between God and himself.

Eventually, the police had to rule out Husselmann as a suspect considering that, for some reason, they could neither confirm nor deny the validity of the DNA evidence. They also believed that the actual B1 Butcher might have tried to frame Husselmann and planted the evidence in his house. Husselmann was previously sentenced for robbing and shooting someone in Rehoboth near the B1 on May 31, 1988, and then stabbed a hotel gatekeeper to death on June 30, 1988. He was 21 at the time.

During his incarceration, Husselmann had shaped himself into a model prisoner, and his psychiatric evaluations suggested that he possessed above-average intelligence. The report did caution that Husselmann also showed signs of being emotionally unstable, proven by his aggressive actions in the murders he committed. Furthermore, the report also suggested that Husselmann had anti-social tendencies. Nevertheless, Husselmann had used his time behind bars to gain higher education as well as some technical qualifications, which allowed him to gain employment at the Windhoek Vocational Training Center as an instructor. He was still working there at the time of his suicide.

Unnamed Suspect

On September 21, 2007, the police arrested a 50-year-old man who claimed to be behind the killing of a woman whose body parts were found in Grootfontein on September 17, 2007. He had apparently confessed to a few people at a supermarket in Otjiwarongo, where he was buying newspapers. This led to the cashier being hospitalized after hyperventilating. It all started when the cashier commented on the gruesome death which had been reported in the newspaper the man was carrying. The man, whose identity was undisclosed, then bragged about murdering and dismembering the victim himself. He also threatened to do the same thing to the cashier. The woman was outraged and apparently in shock but had the foresight to inform her supervisor of what had transpired.

But the man, a resident of Windhoek, continued his bragging as he then went to a pharmacy nearby to repeat the same claims. The police were called in, and they took him into custody. However, there seemed to be no evidence to back his claims, and the interrogation yielded no results. Nevertheless, the police considered charging him for threatening the supermarket cashier.

The Aftermath

The discovery of the severed body parts and the subsequent efforts of the authorities to get to the bottom of these crimes drew widespread criticism against the police for not efficiently dealing with the crisis. The severity of the violence involved in these crimes, not to mention the mistaken identity incident of Jacoba Olivier and the later suicide of Hans Husselmann, did no favors to the police's image.

Around the time the severed limbs were positively identified to be those of Sanna Helena ǁGaroës, several women hailing from Windhoek, Rehoboth, and Tsumis Park came together and issued an open letter in July 2007 addressed to the B1 Butcher. They made an appeal to the killer to turn himself over to the authorities and also to lead them to the discovery of the unaccounted-for body parts so that the families could ensure a decent burial for the victims. No one has yet to come forward.

The fact that the targeted women were sex workers showed some bias on the part of the police in actively pursuing any inquiries, and the abrupt end to the killings—or at least the discovery of any further dismembered body parts—effectively put an end to the investigation.

But the specter of the B1 Butcher will continue to haunt the residents of Windhoek and the surrounding areas, and everyone will think twice before unloading a dumpster on a quiet morning along the wide-open road.

5

THE EASTBOUND STRANGLER

Think of the last time you went on vacation. You can likely recall happy memories of fun-filled escapades, swimming in pristine waters, shopping in fancy malls, and savoring delicious cuisine. Those are the memories one would want from a vacation in an exotic location, where the bustling nightlife adds zest to your otherwise mundane existence that you needed a massive break from in the first place. All you want to do is throw away your worries and jet off to a resort where you can have all of your wishes catered to, or at least make for one fantastic social media album.

The same couldn't be said for the two women in Atlantic City who were just out for a casual stroll one day in 2006. But if they had known that their innocent, unassuming walk would lead to the discovery of four brutally murdered women, they probably would have preferred to stay at home. In just one day, they unearthed the trail of death left behind by the Eastbound Strangler.

The Victims

As mentioned, there are four known victims of the Eastbound Strangler. All were found in a ditch on November 20, 2006, about sixty feet apart from each other. Each was positioned so that they were facing east toward the casinos, which led to the moniker of the "Eastbound Strangler" being assigned to the as-yet-unidentified murderer. The victims were clothed but missing their shoes and socks. All four victims were known sex workers in Atlantic City, and they had been leading troubled and dysfunctional lives, primarily due to their profession and dependency on drugs. Their choice to be sex workers fueled this dangerous habit, which led them into the darkest corners of the city, also known as America's Playground.

There were high levels of designer drugs found in their systems once they were autopsied. Because of the various stages of decomposition of the latter three bodies, the cause of death could not be confirmed. The body of the most recent victim, Kim Raffo, was found only one day after disappearing, and her cause of death was revealed to be strangulation. But apart from their careers and vices, they each had children that were left behind.

Kim Raffo

The destruction in the wake of the Eastbound Strangler's murderous rage was unearthed on the morning of November 20, 2006. The first to be discovered was the body of Kim Raffo, located behind the Golden Key Motel in Egg Harbor Township. The 35-year-old Raffo was lying face down in a drainage ditch in a slew of chemical waste.

After living in Brooklyn all her life, Raffo moved to Atlantic City in 2003 along with her boyfriend, trying to make a new life for herself. However, she was caught in a dangerous substance abuse habit and ended up as a sex worker in Atlantic City. She kept trying to break the habit but was in too deep and continuously relapsed. She also had two children and had even moved to Florida with them, but her drug habit drew her back to her old life in Atlantic City. Raffo was last seen in Atlantic City the morning before she was found. When the police arrived at the scene, they concluded that Raffo had been killed after being strangled by a ligature, presumably a piece of cord or rope.

But that wasn't the only gruesome discovery that day. A short distance away from where Raffo's body was found, the police also discovered not one, not two, but three other female corpses. All of them were at different stages of decomposition, which suggested a gap between the times they were killed. Much like Raffo, they were all face down and barefoot and appeared to have been strangled to death. It was also noticed later that their bodies were all pointing eastward.

Barbara V. Breidor

Forty-two-year-old Barbara Breidor was one of the three corpses found a few yards away from Raffo's body on November 20, 2006. She had disappeared in the middle of October 2006, but no one could recall when they last saw her alive. Her behavior was unpredictable, so she wasn't reported missing until some weeks later. She had been working at the local casinos as a cocktail waitress but was caught up in a crack addiction, and desperate to get her fix, she would pay as much as $300 a day to support the habit. Thus, she became a sex worker.

But her family has always highlighted how Breidor suffered due to domestic abuse and had been depressed following the death of her father. At one point, she even started self-medicating, which ultimately led to her drug addiction. Breidor left behind a 9-year-old daughter.

Tracy Ann Roberts

Originally a resident of Delaware, Tracy Ann Roberts had moved to Atlantic City sometime before her murder. Despite being a trained medical assistant, Roberts was unable to escape the shackles of substance abuse which ultimately led her to a life as a sex worker. Prior to her death, the 23-year-old Roberts had been last seen alive earlier in the same month after she had an altercation with a man who was trying to be her pimp. When she refused, this man attacked her and hit her throat hard enough to send her to the hospital.

Like Breidor, Roberts also left behind a young daughter.

Molly Jean Dilts

The last of the bodies found that day was 20-year-old Molly Jean Dilts. Born and raised in the blue-collar mining town of Black Lick, Pennsylvania, Dilts was said to be a prostitute by one of her acquaintances, though there was no evidence of this on her criminal record. Both her mother and brother had died very early on, which had affected her a great deal. According to the examination, it is estimated that she must have been killed around a month before her body was found, and it was in a terrible state of decomposition. She was identified by the authorities because of an English bulldog tattoo on her body.

The Investigation

So far, detectives have not been able to make any arrests that would prove to be conclusive. The county prosecutor at the time had already deemed this to be the work of a serial killer, with the most obvious sign being that the killer had chosen the exact same spot to dump the bodies. It is still open to debate whether the killer was a local who knew the area very well or a drifter who had the ability to navigate the bustling Atlantic City undetected and unhindered.

There have been no eyewitnesses who saw any vehicles or people near the victims when they were last spotted, and in the case of other sex workers, coming forward with any information could potentially mean putting themselves in the crosshairs of the killer. According to the Sex Workers Outreach Project USA, other sex workers would have thought twice before reporting any sighting or encounter with the killer, primarily out of the fear that they themselves might be charged for solicitation. The police and the public prosecutor did their best to alleviate any such concerns of the community and urged any witnesses to step forward without fear of prejudice.

As there were no further victims found in the same gruesome manner, the police speculated the killer might have been caught and imprisoned for other crimes or perhaps may even be dead. This is based on the theory that as this was apparently the work of a serial killer, they wouldn't have stopped at random. The only reasons for them to cease killing are because they no longer have the ability to do so or have dealt with the underlying causes of why they kill. As the former is not true in the case of Atlantic City, the latter is the only plausible scenario in which the Eastbound Strangler would have stopped. But the police found that highly unlikely.

Though they didn't name any credible suspects, the police had a few leads that were believed to be promising during the course of the investigation.

The Suspects

Terry Oleson

There were many factors that led the police to 41-year-old Oleson. A resident of Alloway, New Jersey, Oleson was a handyman living in the Golden Key Motel in exchange for repairing the motel's toilets and sinks. Located around 60 miles away from his house in Alloway, it also had a reputation for being a haven for sex workers who brought clients there around the time of the killings.

Oleson was first implicated in the killings after his girlfriend saw the victims' bodies on the news. She then called the police and claimed that Oleson was the killer. The police brought him in for questioning and also searched his house in Alloway. They were alarmed at several hidden video cameras present in the home, which were being used for voyeuristic activities. One of them had footage of a teenage girl—the daughter of

Olesen's girlfriend—in her room and in different stages of undress.

During their investigation of Oleson, which lasted up to eight hours without his attorney present, Olesen maintained his innocence and declared that he was being set up by his girlfriend. Apparently, they were about to break up soon due to a domestic dispute, and she was only getting back at him. According to Olesen, the police were adamant that he had killed the four victims. When presented with the hidden camera footage of his former girlfriend's teenage daughter, he claimed that he was unaware of it but later pleaded guilty to a charge of invasion of privacy.

However, there was no conclusive evidence tying Olesen to any of the bodies found outside Atlantic City. He had submitted his DNA samples, but there were no traces found on the bodies to compare them to.

Eldred Raymond Burchell

Another person of interest in the case was a drifter named Eldred Raymond Burchell, who had a habit of referring to himself as "The River Man." This was a reference to "The Green River Killer," a moniker given to Gary Ridgway, who was responsible for killing at least 71 women during the 1980s and 1990s in the State of Washington. Most of these victims were also sex workers.

Eldred was implicated when a woman named Denise Hill claimed that Burchell had confessed to killing people and was in Atlantic City around the time the murders took place. Hill, herself a sex worker, claimed that Burchell spent time with her within that timeframe, and his claims made her suspect that he was the man responsible. However, before the police could capitalize on this information, Burchell had skipped town and could not be found again.

Parallels to the Long Island Serial Killer

Between May 2010 and April 2011, at least ten people were murdered in Suffolk County, New York, most of them sex workers and killed by strangulation. The Gilgo Beach Serial Killer's victims were found on Gilgo Beach and Oak Beach and took place just under 170 miles away from Atlantic City. A documentary movie theorized that the Long Island Serial Killer was, in fact, the Eastbound Strangler, considering the similarities and that whoever had committed those murders in Atlantic City could have turned their attention to Long Island four years later.

This killing spree began when 24-year-old Shannan Gilbert disappeared from Gilgo Beach after leaving a client's house in May of 2010. During the search, aided by sniffer dogs, the police uncovered the body of a different woman near a thicket. The search continued, which led to the discovery of three other bodies within walking distance of each other over the next few days. All four were women later identified as sex workers.

The first to be found was 24-year-old Melissa Barthelemy, who had vanished on July 12, 2009. A resident of the Bronx, her body was discovered on December 13, 2010, along with that of 27-year-old Amber Lynn Costello, who had gone missing on September 2, 2010. The third body found on the same day was that of 22-year-old Megan Waterman. She had disappeared on June 6, 2010, leaving behind a daughter. But still, there was no sign of Shannan Gilbert.

Many months later, the skull of a woman was discovered on Suffolk County beaches in March 2011, later identified as belonging to 20-year-old sex worker Jessica Taylor. More bodies would be found throughout the spring as the total count reached ten, eight of them women, one man, and also a toddler.

It wouldn't be until December 2011 when Shannan Gilbert's body was finally discovered in the marshes of Oak Beach. This was roughly three miles away from where all the other bodies had been found. According to the police, Gilbert appeared to have drowned entirely by accident as she was under the influence of drugs, which led to them excluding her from the others. Gilbert's mother, however, has rejected such theories and commissioned an independent autopsy of her daughter. This autopsy suggests that Gilbert had also been strangled like the previous victims.

Much like the Eastbound Strangler, there has been no suspect named in connection with the Long Island Serial Killer victims. Moreover, the investigators do not consider the killings that took place in Long Island to be connected with those in Atlantic City. Thus, The Eastbound Strangler remains free and unaccounted for to this day.

6

THE PARAQUAT KILLER

Most serial killers use the same method to kill their victims, and in the same vein, their deliberate procedures allow them to derive pleasure from killing their victims. Strangulation with ligatures lets them see the life slip out of their victims' eyes, as does asphyxiation. Stabbing them or beating them to death allows the serial killer to exert the rage-filled impulses that they usually keep in check. Killers see the fear in their victims' eyes when they attack in close quarters. The victims know that death is at hand, which only inflates the killer's superiority complex.

However, one would never expect a serial killer to employ a method of poisoning victims at random using fun-filled flavored drinks from something as subtle as vending machines. But in 1985, one such killer terrorized the country of Japan as he mixed the deadly insecticide known as Paraquat to kill 12 unsuspecting victims who bought themselves death in a bottle.

This is the story of the Paraquat Killer.

The Method

The Paraquat Killer was unique in the method he used to carry out 12 murders throughout 1985. His victims were entirely chosen at random from those who picked up an unclaimed drink from a vending machine. The killer relied on the tradition of the Japanese people to not let any unclaimed beverage go to waste. Furthermore, the prominence of vending machines in modern Japanese culture and lifestyle was and continues to be massive, as people bought all sorts of food and drink from vending machines, such as pizza, hot soup, ice cream, and soft drinks. They are so in vogue that women can even use a vending machine to buy new underwear.

But unknown to these people, the drinks had been left there deliberately and were tampered with to contain the fatal herbicide known as Paraquat. It is a toxic chemical that is still used in some weed killers even though it is banned in several countries. Paraquat is highly poisonous and harmful even to the touch. It can cause chemical burns within the blood vessel walls stemming from a combination of erythema, blistering, and hemorrhagic diabrosis. It is utterly lethal if ingested and causes rapid inflammation around major blood vessel tissues. It has even been known to burn holes in a human throat, resulting in a swift but agonizing death.

Once Paraquat enters the kidneys, the body no longer has any means to remove it, which results in the rest of the organs shutting down, most notably the lungs. As Paraquat is attracted to areas with more oxygen, the lungs are the obvious target, and it leads to pulmonary fibrosis. The lungs fill up with liquid, which makes it feel as if the victim is drowning in a matter of hours.

Even though Paraquat is banned in several countries, it is still used in the US by licensed professionals. However, they are still at significant risk of Paraquat exposure even if they do not ingest it. Long-term exposure to Paraquat can have detrimental effects on one's health. It can lead to Parkinson's disease, heart disease, kidney failure, respiratory difficulties due to lung inflammation and esophageal scarring, as well as reproductive problems.

But the Paraquat Killer's designs weren't limited to making people suffer for an extended period of time; he wanted them to die horrible, agonizing deaths as soon as possible. Even though he wasn't there to see the life leave their eyes as most serial killers do, the Paraquat Killer's intentions were nothing but brutal and sadistic.

The Victims

One major component behind the success of the Paraquat Killer was his reliance on the good nature of the Japanese people. Their habits of not letting things go to waste resulted in so many people not questioning why a drink was in the dispensing slot unclaimed; they would simply pick it up and consume it. There was also a cultural fad of paying it forward where a consumer could pay for an extra drink and leave it to be claimed by whoever stopped by next.

Most of the beverages containing the Paraquat poison were, in fact, Oronamin C. This worked perfectly for the killer, as he had the means to deliver death to his victims for the price of only a few Yen. As if that weren't enough, the company behind Oronamin C was running a special promotion that automatically dispensed a free Oronamin C bottle with every purchase as a marketing tactic. This caught the unsuspecting public off guard, and they figured that the extra drink was genuinely free.

Victim #1: *Unnamed Truck Driver*

The first known fatality transpired after a truck driver bought a drink out of a vending machine in Fukuyama, Hiroshima. On April 30, 1985, while he was waiting for the beverage, he was also offered a complimentary bottle of a popular supplement called Oronamin C, which was being promoted by the Otsuka Pharmaceutical Company. The truck driver did not think too much of it and consumed the free bottle of Oronamin C.

The driver was then immediately rushed to a hospital, where he died a month later, on May 30, 1985. The analysis of his vomit showed traces of the banned weed killer known as Paraquat, and it appeared to have come from the Oronamin C that he had consumed. Based on the deadly effects of Paraquat ingestion, the 45-year-old truck driver holding out for a month simply prolonged the inevitable.

But he would only be the first as the rest of the year would see even more death as Paraquat destroyed 11 other Japanese people throughout the country by the end of 1985 in what also began to be known as the Vending Machine Murders.

Victim #2

The month of September would mark the highest number of fatalities at the hands of the Paraquat Killer as a 52-year-old bought a bottle of Oronamin C from a vending machine on September 11, 1985, and found another one inside the machine ready to be taken. He drank both of them but immediately started succumbing to the deadly poison. The beverage samples were found to contain Paraquat, and the man died on September 14, 1985.

Victim #3

The very next day after victim two bought the fatal beverage, a college student visited a vending machine on September 12, 1985, to buy an energy drink called Real Gold. Interestingly, there was a bottle of Real Gold already available in the dispensing slot. It appears that it must have been purchased by another patron but had not dispensed on time. Traditionally, Japanese citizens do not let any drinks go to waste, and so the victim picked up the dispensed bottle as well as the one purchased. He had both of them once he got home, and then died two days later on September 14, 1985, at the age of 22. While the means of death and the modus operandi were the same, this was an anomaly as the poison used to kill this victim was Diquat instead of Paraquat. Nevertheless, his murder is also counted on the Vending Machine Murders list.

Victim #4

A few days after victim three's death, a 30-year-old discovered an unclaimed cola can underneath a vending machine on September 19, 1985. Following the same Japanese habits, he drank the cola, which led to his death on September 22, 1985, at the hospital where he was being treated. Paraquat traces were found in both the cola can and his stomach contents.

Victim #5

The very next day after victim four was poisoned, a 45-year-old went over to a vending machine on September 20, 1985, to buy a drink but found that there were not one but two bottles of the Real Gold energy drink already waiting in the dispensing slot. Thinking nothing of it, he took both beverages home and drank them right away. He died on September 22, 1985, with Paraquat discovered in the drink bottles.

Victim #6

A 50-year-old was the next to go as he found two bottles of Oronamin C in a vending machine on September 23, 1985, ready to be picked up. However, he did not drink them immediately; instead, he took them home and drank them two days later. He died on October 7, 1985, with Paraquat poisoning the cause of death as per the analysis of the beverage samples.

This was the fifth and final poisoning of September 1985, but the Paraquat Killer's reign of terror was far from over.

Victim #7

Similar to victim six, a 44-year-old bought a bottle of Oronamin C on October 5, 1985, and was killed by Paraquat poisoning on October 21, 1985. The poison traces were found in the beverage samples.

Victim #8

On October 15, 1985, a 69-year-old found two unidentified drinks in a vending machine ready to be picked up. He took them home and, after drinking them, died on November 13, 1985, due to Paraquat poisoning.

Victim #9

Another case of an unidentified drink from a vending machine led to the poisoning death of a 55-year-old on October 21, 1985.

Victim #10

Paraquat poisoning in Oronamin C had become a visible pattern by now as it caused the death of a 50-year-old on October 28, 1985. He found a bottle of the drink in a vending machine dispensing slot and did not want to waste it. This was the fourth and final Paraquat poisoning in October 1985, but there would be two more murders before the terror of the Paraquat Killer came to an abrupt halt.

Victim #11

On November 7, 1985, a male bought a bottle of Oronamin C but found two more bottles of the same beverage already dispensed by the vending machine. With three Oronamin C bottles, the 42-year-old went back home and drank the two free ones first, which resulted in his death on November 16, 1985, from Paraquat poisoning.

Victim #12

The twelfth and final victim of the Paraquat Killer was a 17-year-old who, on November 17, 1985, got a free cola while buying another drink from the vending machine. She died a week later with traces of Paraquat found in the beverage.

The Investigation

Despite working around the clock, the police made very little headway in identifying any suspects behind the Vending Machine Killings. The Paraquat Killer had apparently chosen those particular vending machines for their presence in areas with very little traffic, not to mention that Closed-Circuit TV Cameras (CCTV) and other forms of video surveillance were virtually non-existent. Despite a hands-on approach with the way he poisoned a wide variety of drinks, the killer also took great care not to leave any DNA evidence behind.

Furthermore, the police could not even get a clue as to the motive of the killer. No one had come forward to claim responsibility for the killings, and the vending machines were selected at considerable distances from each other with no link. There was no way to suggest that the murder victims had been chosen beforehand, and it appears that the killer had targeted people indiscriminately. Moreover, the use of DNA profiling in investigating crimes had only just gotten started with limited methods available. Interestingly, sometime before the Paraquat Killer had commenced his vicious spree of murders, there had been a series of threats directed at the public. However, no one could have expected the killer to choose vending machines and Paraquat as the murder weapon.

The last known victim of the Paraquat Killer may have been killed in November 1985, but the poisonings seemed to be far from over. It was reported in the news that copycat incidents had started taking place in December 1985. In one case, unknown persons had left containers of tainted milk in schools located in the Mie Prefecture. Also, other poisoned drinks laced with sulfur and lime led to two more cases of poisoning in Tokyo, and other people also used Paraquat to commit suicide.

However, much like the actual Paraquat Killer, these incidents also remain unsolved, and the cases went cold.

The Suspects

The Monster With 21 Faces

As supplementary victims of the Vending Machine Killings, a wide variety of drink manufacturers and distributors, as well as vending machine distributors' products, were tampered with and used to murder unsuspecting Japanese civilians. Sadly, this wasn't the first time that criminals had targeted fast-moving food product makers. A year before the Paraquat Killer struck, a mysterious gang of criminals calling themselves the "Monster With 21 Faces" started sending threatening letters to the Glico Company, followed by other food companies, news agencies, and the police on May 10, 1984. In those letters, they aimed to create a public panic by declaring that they had allegedly left cyanide-laced candies at various locations which were easy for children to find.

The moniker of The Monster With 21 Faces was inspired by a series of Japanese detective novels, and the namesake was the villain from the series. The letters kept coming during 1985, which is when the Vending Machine Killings started. By then, the police had begun to turn their attention to these killings, and for some reason, the letters also stopped coming in. More than likely, the killings appear to have been inspired by the Monster With 21 Faces, and the notes had only been circulating to create public panic and gain notoriety. However, the Paraquat Killer took it a step further by poisoning drinks and claiming 12 lives. In either case, there were no demands made by either party.

The Monster With 21 Faces concluded their reign of inciting terror when the police superintendent investigating the case, Yamamoto, committed suicide. With the pressure of the issue too great for him to bear, he took his own life by self-immolation, or lighting himself on fire. Soon after Yamamoto's death, a final letter arrived from The Monster With 21 Faces, saying: "We decided to forget about tormenting food companies... We are bad guys. That means we've got more to do than bullying companies. It's fun to lead a bad guy's life" (Giacomazzo, 2021).

The Yukaihan

There was another theory put forward by psychologists that the Paraquat Killer was, in fact, one of many thrill-seekers and sociopaths who held no value to human life and would feel superior at inflicting pain and suffering upon hapless victims. These thrill-seekers, or *yukaihan* as they are called, relish the image of seeing total strangers in agony and suffering, which makes Paraquat poisoning an ideal method for them to achieve this sadistic pleasure. But with no actual suspects coming forward to take responsibility for the crimes and with no progress made by the police, the theory simply remains a theory.

The Aftermath

Naturally, after such violent incidents began gripping the population of Japan with fear, the manufacturers and distributors of the drinks started to take preventive measures to ensure public safety. The most immediate step was taken by vending machine operators as well as the Japan Soft Drink Bottlers' Association, who started placing warning stickers on their machines which discouraged the public from drinking any unclaimed drinks they found and either disposing of them in the trash or reporting it to the police. Around 1.3 million warning stickers were placed, which greatly helped to reduce the number of such poisonings (Haberman, 1985). Furthermore, the manufacturers of Oronamin C, Otsuka Pharmaceuticals, came up with a new design for their bottle caps where they replaced the existing screw caps with pull tabs which helped to reduce tampering. Unfortunately, other manufacturers and members of the Japan Soft Drink Bottlers' Association held the view that the onus was on the customers to be extra careful and notice if there were any signs of tampering.

There appeared to be a resurgence of poisoned drinks popping up in vending machine slots in 1998; however, as with the Paraquat Killer, no one came forward to claim responsibility. Furthermore, there are limited details on whether Paraquat was used in those poisonings or if it was a completely different chemical. There is every possibility that these incidents were caused by someone influenced by the original Paraquat Killer, or perhaps it was actually the Paraquat Killer himself.

In 2010, Japan abolished the statute of limitations for murder investigations. If the killer ever comes forward or is identified, they will be deemed liable and are open to prosecution for the crimes. If the authorities ever unearth the identity of the Paraquat Killer, it leaves the chance for justice to be served.

7

THE MAD BUTCHER OF KINGSBURY RUN

The following is the tale of the Mad Butcher of Kingsbury Run, who slaughtered 12 men and women from 1935 to 1938 and hacked them in ways far too depraved for society to bear. He targeted the homeless, the outcasts, the sex workers, and many others who were down on their luck after The Great Depression and made their last moments on Earth an agonizing hell. The Mad Butcher ensured that many of them could not be identified, as he decapitated the victims, and most of their heads were never recovered. But in almost all cases, the victims would be found torso-first, which earned them the unfortunate moniker of "The Cleveland Torso Murders."

The Method

The level of barbarity that the Mad Butcher of Kingsbury Run operated at was unparalleled at that point in the early 20th century. According to the investigation into the murders, the killer appeared to have had tremendous strength to carry out decapitations and dismemberments of human bodies, as well as detailed knowledge of the human anatomy. The manner of the cuts inflicted on the victims' bodies showed finesse and tremendous skill. The most likely reason for this could be that the killer had previously been a medical practitioner or perhaps a butcher or a hunter. It is also believed that the killer had committed the murders at a different location and then managed to dump parts of the bodies elsewhere, primarily dumping them in the drains. This meant that not only was he strong enough to transport all of those human remains at considerable distances, but he also knew how to navigate around the erratically populated area of Kingsbury Run without being noticed or suspected of anything out of the ordinary.

Above all else, the killer was indeed a highly intelligent psychopath. He was a fully equipped killer who carefully planned the murders and picked out his victims after proper observation and went to great lengths to ensure that they could not be identified. Most of the corpses had been decapitated, and in many cases, the hands and arms were not found and therefore could not provide fingerprint identification. He also had the tools needed to perform the decapitations and mutilations and may even have had access to a cold-storage area.

The Victims

Due to the fact that most of the victims could not be identified, there is no conclusive evidence of whether they had any connection with each other or the killer. However, the Mad Butcher had pretty specific criteria when it came to choosing his victims. Those that were identified were mostly drifters or dwellers of Kingsbury Run, mainly hailing from the notorious Roaring Third. They were either poor, destitute, and down on their luck or were also working in the Roaring Third at low-end jobs, such as waiters and sex workers. At least one of the men was rumored to be homosexual, so there is every possibility that his murder could have been a hate crime, as evidenced by the mutilation of the victim's genitals in that case. But again, many victims could not be identified as their heads were never found. Based on the psychopathic profile of the killer, there is every possibility that he kept the heads as a trophy of his gruesome exploits.

Victim Zero: The Lady of the Lake

The torso of a young woman with the thighs still attached was found on the shores of Lake Erie near Bratenahl on September 5, 1934. The legs had been amputated at the knees, and the skin itself had taken on a leathery and tough complexion due to an unknown chemical preservative. A search was carried out, yielding the discovery of a few more body parts. It appeared that the woman was in her mid-30s but could not be identified and was only known as "The Lady of the Lake." Though she was thought to be a one-off case, it would take two more years until she was included as victim zero in the trail of death by the Mad Butcher of Kingsbury Run.

Victim #1: Edward Andrassy and Victim #2: Unidentified Male

Around a year later, the body of a Caucasian male was found at the bottom of Jackass Hill near Kingsbury Run on September 23, 1935. It was discovered by two teenage boys who were shocked and horrified at its condition. The body was naked with only socks on, and the wrists had signs of rope burns. Moreover, the body appeared to have been drained of blood and had also been cleaned before being left there. But the worst of all was that the head was missing, as were the penis and the testicles. According to the coroner, the cause of death was due to the decapitation, and he had been killed two or three days prior to being found. When the police conducted their search nearby, they found a second body of a Caucasian male, around the age of 40, which was similarly decapitated and emasculated. Traces of the same chemical preservative found on The Lady of the Lake were also found on this second body, and it appeared to have been left there for at least a few weeks.

The fingerprints of the first body found in September 1935 revealed his identity to be 28-year-old Edward Andrassy. He had a prior criminal record and was frequently sighted at the bars and other establishments at the Roaring Third. It was also claimed that Andrassy was homosexual. The identity of the second body remains a mystery; however, the manner in which the beheading and emasculation took place, along with the chemical preservative used in the corpse of the unidentified male and The Lady of the Lake, made it clear that there was a definite link. This was when the investigation started, and Andrassy was officially named victim number one.

Victim #3: Florence Polillo

Over three months after Andrassy's body was discovered along with that of an unidentified male, the half-body of a female wrapped in newspaper and placed in two baskets was found by a woman on January 26, 1936, just outside the premises of Hart Manufacturing on Central Avenue. It took another ten days to recover the rest of the body, with the exception of the head, which was never found. The other remains were found in a nearby vacant lot on Orange Avenue. Her identity was confirmed to be of a waitress and barmaid named Florence Polillo, who also worked as a prostitute in the Roaring Third and lived along the outskirts of the area. Much like Andrassy and the unidentified male corpse, Polillo had been killed by decapitation about two to four days before being located.

Victim #4: The Tattooed Man

Six months later, the head and body of a yet-to-be-identified Caucasian male were discovered in Kingsbury Run on June 5, 1936. The head was found near the East 55th Street bridge by two boys, wrapped in a pair of trousers. The rest of the body was dumped outside of a police building. The cause of death was decapitation once again, and the victim had been killed a couple of days prior. The body had also been drained of blood and cleaned, just like Andrassy. There were six different tattoos all over the body, but even with these and the victim's fingerprints, the police couldn't make a positive identification. Thus the moniker of "The Tattooed Man."

In an unusual occurrence, the victim's head was reproduced in plaster, and his tattoos were also re-made as a diagram. Both of which were then displayed at the 1936 Great Lakes Exposition. "The Death Mask" and the tattoo chart were viewed then by over 100,000 visitors, and the death mask itself is still displayed at the Cleveland Police Museum.

Victim #5

The very next month, the headless body of a 40-year-old Caucasian male was discovered in the woods near

Big Creek. The victim appeared to have been dead for around two months when a teenage girl passing through the woods came upon it on July 22, 1936. Upon further searches of the area, the authorities found the head and some bloody clothing a short distance away. It appears that the victim had been killed on the spot as there was a great deal of blood that had seeped into the ground at the exact location where the body was placed. The victim was never identified.

Victim #6

On September 10, 1936, around two years after The Lady of the Lake was discovered, the upper half of a man's torso was found accidentally by someone who was passing through the town as he tripped over it in a hurry to catch a train. When the police arrived, they began searching for more clues at a pool close to the body. This 'pool' turned out to be an open sewer. From there, the lower half of the torso and partial remains of both legs were recovered. Optimistic that the rest of the remains were in that sewer, the police sent in a diver to scour through it for any other body parts. Based on what they had found, the victim appeared to be in his late 20s and was killed by decapitation. According to the coroner, the manner of the beheading suggests that the killer used one strong and clean stroke to sever the head from the body and appeared to have intimate knowledge of the human anatomy. The death from such a strike would have been instantaneous. The victim was killed a couple of days before the remains were found, and he was never identified.

With the sixth such brutal slaying and no suspects, the local newspapers began running the story of "The Mad Butcher of Kingsbury Run," which gripped the imagination and fear of the public at large. The diver's search for the remains of the victim in the sewer was reported to have been witnessed by around 600 onlookers. The coroner who examined these bodies brought together a group of other experts as well as the police to attempt to create a profile of the person behind these gruesome murders. The newspapers began to refer to this group as the "torso clinic."

Victim #7

By November 1936, the mayor was re-elected, but a new coroner arrived at the scene who appeared to be a lot more zealous and knowledgeable, with an understanding of medicine as well as a degree in law. Nevertheless, the killings continued, and brutally hacked corpses kept popping up. On the shores along Bratenahl, the upper half of a torso belonging to a woman in her mid-20s was found by a man on February 23, 1937. This time, the death was not by decapitation, as it appears to have been done after she was killed. The coroner estimated the murder to have taken place at least three to four days prior. Three months later, the lower half of the torso washed ashore. However, no identification has ever been made.

Victim #8: Rose Wallace

That summer, a human skull was found along with a burlap sack containing skeletal remains below the Lorain-Carnegie bridge on June 6, 1937. Examination revealed that the remains were that of a 40-year-old petite African American woman, and her dental records unofficially confirmed the identity of Scovill Avenue resident Rose Wallace. She appeared to have been killed a year earlier. Curiously, one of her rib bones had been removed.

Victim #9

In July 1937, a great deal of unrest was prevalent in the Flats due to ongoing labor disputes. As a result, the National Guard had been stationed throughout the town. One of the guardsmen was observing a tugboat from over the West 3rd Street bridge when he spotted a body part in the boat's wake in the Cuyahoga River on July 6, 1937. The police began to recover the rest of the body, but only the head could not be located. This corpse belonged to a man in his late-30s and appeared to have been brutalized even more, as the heart had been ripped out and the abdomen had been disemboweled. Much like the previous victims, this man had been killed two to three days before being discovered.

Victim #10

The Cuyahoga River would see another victim a year later when a piece of a woman's lower leg washed up on the shore. It was spotted on April 8, 1938, by a laborer heading to work who mistook it for a dead fish. The police searched around the area, and it took them a month, but they found two burlap sacks from the river. These sacks contained two parts of a torso and most of the remains of both legs. But no arms meant no hands, meaning no fingerprints, and the victim could not be identified. The post-mortem examination revealed that the victim had been drugged, possibly by the killer, though it is also likely that the victim could have been an addict. The murder appeared to have occurred three to five days prior.

Victims #11 and #12

The last two victims were found at a dumpsite on August 16, 1938, by some scrap collectors. The first torso was wrapped in a men's blazer, which was then wrapped in an old quilt. Meanwhile, a woman's arms and legs were found wrapped in brown paper tied with rubber bands and placed in a makeshift box that had been built recently. This time, the head was also found wrapped in brown paper. Neither victim could be identified, though the coroner believed that victim #11 appeared to have been refrigerated. The coroner estimated the time of the murder around four to six months earlier.

The Investigation

After the discovery of victim six, two full-time detectives scoured through the Kingsbury Run underworld, focusing mainly on the Roaring Third. Over the course of different bodies being discovered every year, these two alone had questioned over 1,500 people compared to the 5,000 overall by the entire department, making it the most extensive police investigation in the history of Cleveland. The officers would often disguise themselves in order to fit into the town's seedy underbelly.

The case also gained prominence with the involvement of Eliot Ness, the man responsible for bringing noted gangster Al Capone to trial in 1931 and also for enforcing Prohibition laws in Chicago in 1932. He had been appointed as Director of the Department for Public Safety for Cleveland, Ohio, and had oversight of the police department, which made the case of The Mad Butcher of Kingsbury Run under his watchful eye. But things escalated when victims eleven and twelve were found in a scrapyard that was in full view of Ness's office window.

No longer wanting to allow the safety of the public to be jeopardized, Ness authorized a full-scale raid of the Roaring Third at 12:40 in the morning of August 18, 1938, with 35 police officers and detectives, 11 squad cars, two vans, and three fire trucks. Their aim was to target the slum dwellings and shacks behind the Public Square where the Cuyahoga River twists. The raid started from the South, working its way up, and they picked 63 men for questioning. The police and firefighters then conducted a thorough search of the abandoned dwellings to find any clues related to the Torso Murders by the time dawn broke.

But in a brazen move, Eliot Ness then ordered all the shacks and shanties to be burnt down, which terrified the public even further. It brought down Ness's stock a great deal from the heroic zenith it had risen to in Chicago. Though the press criticized Ness's flagrant use of power, the killings seemed to have stopped right after.

The Suspects

Dr. Francis 'Frank' E. Sweeney

Dr. Sweeney was first named as the killer by Eliot Ness in 1938 and was personally interviewed by Ness. On the day of the interrogation, Ness and the authorities had to stash Dr. Sweeney in a hotel room for three days due to him being excessively drunk. Once he sobered up, Dr. Sweeney was interrogated, and he took two polygraph tests, both of which he failed. The tests were conducted by an expert in polygraph examinations who was confident that Sweeney was the killer. But there was a problem: Dr. Sweeney was the first cousin of Congressman Martin L. Sweeney, who allegedly used his influence to get him a deal.

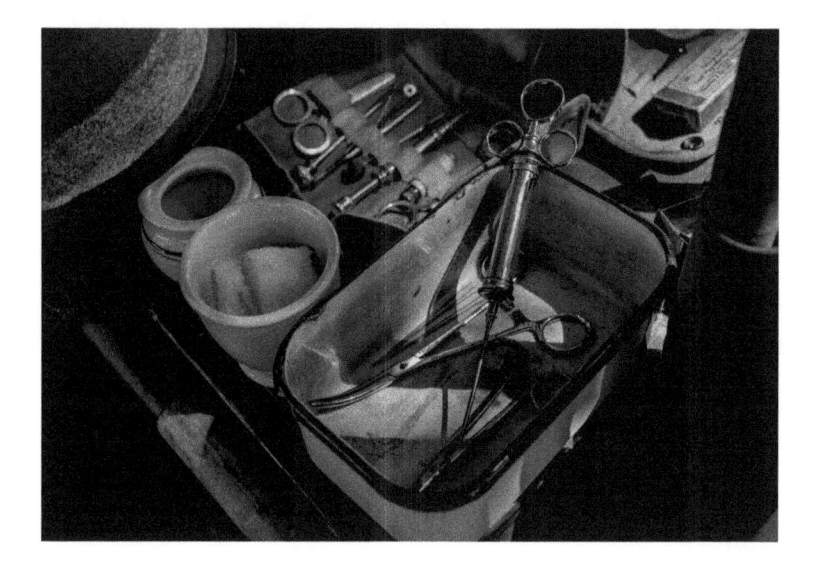

Dr. Sweeney was born on May 5, 1894, and had served in WWI as a medic who was part of a unit that conducted amputations, which matched the earlier assessment that the Torso Killer would be well-versed in human anatomy. However, Dr. Sweeney was discharged for being "25% disabled," according to the notation. He then resumed his practice but was plagued with depression and pathological anxiety brought upon by his experience in the war, for which he turned to alcohol. He was also discharged from his medical practice after he claimed that his wife was an alcoholic in 1933 and committed her for treatment. They were divorced in 1936. When Ness named him a primary suspect, the court ordered him to undergo two psychiatric evaluations in 1938, both of which found him sane.

Dr. Sweeney then avoided any further prosecution by getting committed to a mental institution for veterans. From there, he sent threatening postcards straight to Ness, mocking him for his inability to "get him" and the investigation into the Torso Murders. Ness continued to receive postcards with threats to his family well into the 1950s. Dr. Sweeney made a brief appearance in public in 1939 but quickly returned to the institution until his eventual death on July 9, 1964. The postcards stopped arriving immediately after.

Frank Dolezal

A 52-year-old bricklayer named Frank Dolezal was arrested in July 1939 by the county sheriff in connection with the murder of Florence Polillo. Dolezal and

Polillo had lived together for some time, and as it emerged from the investigation, he also had some interactions with Edward Andrassy and Rose Wallace. Dolezal was also an alcoholic.

But six weeks after he was arrested, Dolezal was found hanged to death inside his cell at the Cuyahoga County Jail. The noose was roughly six feet off the floor. According to the autopsy, Dolezal also had six broken ribs which had been inflicted while he was in custody. This was corroborated by his friends, who claimed that he did not have those injuries at the time of his arrest. Furthermore, Dolezal's supposed confession felt as if he had been told what to say. He gave precise details about the murder and stated that he had killed Polillo in self-defense, not to mention also killing Andrassy. He also made various other nonsensical rants.

However, Dolezal then recanted his confession and claimed that it had been beaten out of him by the police. This occurred shortly before his death under suspicious circumstances. It was very unlikely that Dolezal was the killer, and there is no explanation why the sheriff believed him to be a suspect.

The Aftermath

With no further leads or suspects since 1939, the case went cold. However, there was a slew of future incidents that harkened back to the Mad Butcher of Kingsbury Run. For instance, three corpses were discovered on May 3, 1940, near Pittsburgh, Pennsylvania, in boxcars. The bodies had been hacked to pieces, and the cause of death was decapitation. Several other bodies, both hacked to pieces and decapitated, were discovered between 1939 and 1942, dumped in Pennsylvania swamps. The victims could not be identified.

Then in 1947, the body of a woman was found in Leimert Park, located in Los Angeles. She had also been cut in half, and her body had been drained of all blood. Furthermore, she had also been disemboweled, and there were no intestines. Most of these were hallmarks of the Mad Butcher of Kingsbury Run, and the woman was called the "Black Dahlia" until she was identified as Elizabeth Short. Much like the victims of the Torso Murderer, Elizabeth Short's killer has never been found. This also coincidentally took place in the same year as Eliot Ness's campaign for the mayor of Cleveland, which he did not win. Whether or not Short's murder had any bearing on this is anyone's guess.

As for Ness, his life began to take a downward turn toward the end as, in a cruel irony, he himself fell victim to a severe alcohol consumption problem. He died in 1957 at the age of 54, a shell of his former self. He had dedicated the last few decades to the relentless pursuit of the Mad Butcher of Kingsbury Run and to seeking justice for the 12 victims found along the Cuyahoga River. He was given full police honors at his funeral in Cleveland, and his ashes were scattered near Kingsbury Run, perhaps with the hope of being there if and when the identity of the killer is finally revealed.

8

THE BELIZE RIPPER

Trouble in paradise couldn't be more cliche. But in a country that is a perpetual oasis surrounded by a wide variety of marine and terrestrial wildlife, a viper entered into the midst of the once peaceful and harmonious Belize and preyed upon its most vulnerable inhabitants: the children. With a population of well under half a million people and a land area of around 9,000 square miles, roughly amounting to 30 times smaller than the State of Texas, the killing of four innocent underage girls in the Central American country from 1998 to 2000 plunged the area into a despair that it has never fully recovered from.

All because of one ruthless individual, a man known only as the Belize Ripper.

The Method

In 2000, a forensic pathologist named Dr. Mario Estradabran confirmed after the autopsies that the Belize Ripper had used drugs and alcohol to sedate the victims before killing them. Moreover, the killer used similar tools and weapons to stab the victims and carry out the mutilations, which also suggests that the killer had medical expertise as well as medical instruments. He specifically pointed to the wounds on the neck, which appeared to be puncture wounds and the likely cause of death. The others seemed to be slicing and superficial wounds.

The Victims

Sherilee Nicholas & Jay Blades

The first child to go missing was a fifth-grader named Sherilee Nicholas. She went to school as usual on the morning of September 8, 1998, but never returned. Her mother was the first to see that she was missing, as Sherilee would be home from school when her mother returned from work. Sherilee's mother, June Gabourel, panicked even more when she saw that the rest of her siblings were home, but 13-year-old Sherilee wasn't. She knew that her daughter was not one to skip school or wander off elsewhere, so she felt that something was definitely wrong. When June went over to the Wesly Upper School, located in the southern portion of Belize City, she was told by a teacher that Sherilee wasn't there.

It wouldn't be until a month later when the body of a young girl was found near the George Price Highway on October 9, 1998. The police notified Gabourel, who went to the location where the body had been found in a pool of water. There was no doubt in Gabourel's mind that the corpse was that of her daughter Sherilee, and she was horrified at the state of it. The child had been killed with multiple stab wounds—over 40 of them in her head and chest. Her face had also been cut open, and one of her arms had been severed.

While the sight of Sherilee's brutalized corpse showed her mother how much she had suffered, even more horrifying discoveries were made in the autopsy. Sherilee's body showed obvious signs of rape prior to her death. Moreover, her body was clothed, but she was not wearing the same dress as the day she left. The clothes turned out to be those of another missing girl named Jay Blades. Blades' skull was found along with a few other bones, and so was the knapsack belonging to Sherilee Nicholas. The nine-year-old Blades had disappeared two days before Sherilee's body was found, and she wouldn't be located until six months later.

Sherilee was the oldest of four children who June Gabourel looked after with her meager earnings as a street sweeper. They lived in the poorest part of Belize City, and their neighborhood mainly consisted of modest wooden and concrete houses. Sherilee was described by her fourth-grade teacher as a happy child who enjoyed having conversations and loved math and reading.

Jackie Fern Malic

Six months after Sherilee Nicholas went missing, another girl named Jackie Fern Malic disappeared. On the morning of March 23, 1999, one of her neighbors named Michael Williams offered Jackie and her sister Adelma a ride to school. Even though they were running late and Jackie had said that they should accept the offer, Adelma recalls refusing due to a bad gut feeling, and they made it to school on their own. She was at her school and playing in the playground during recess but was not seen alive again. When Adelma came looking for Jackie once school was over, her teacher told her that Jackie did not return to class after recess. Adelma also recalls that another girl they frequently traveled to school with said to them that there was a man in a car outside the school asking for Jackie. Adelma then rushed home to tell her grandmother, after which they all started looking.

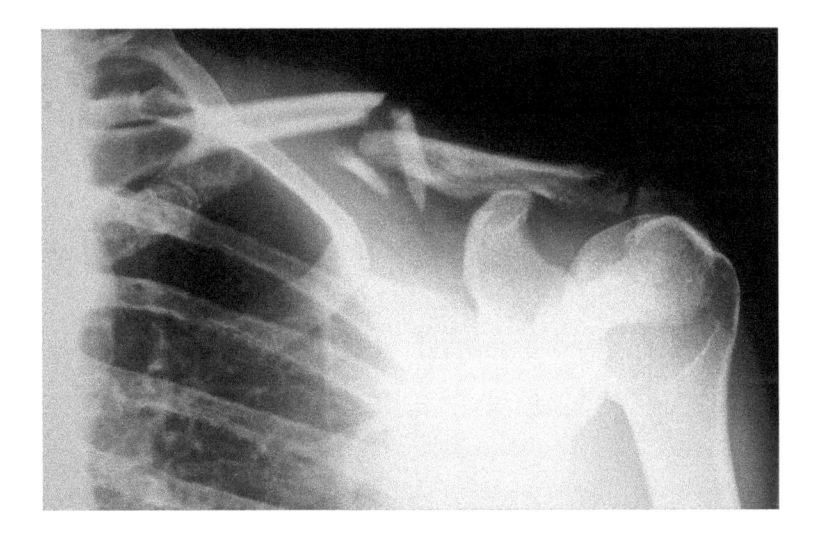

Her body was found two days later in an area that bordered the location where the police had found the body of Sherilee Nicholas. It was placed face down in a puddle near a dirt road. Much like Sherilee, Jackie had also received multiple stab wounds, and her left arm had been cut off. There were also signs that a car had run over her.

Erica Wills

The third girl to vanish in similar circumstances was Erica Wills. She was supposed to be staying overnight with some relatives on June 26, 1999, but when she didn't turn up, they assumed that she had changed her mind and was at home. Tragically, her family had thought that she, in fact, had gone over to her relatives as planned. It wasn't until three days later that they realized eight-year-old Erica was missing. Nearly a month later, on July 18, 1999, a skeletonized body was found behind a quarry in western Belize City. The skull and bones had been picked clean by vultures. Her mother, Karen Wills, identified it as that of her daughter Erica. She recognized some articles of clothing, such as a hairband and a prized Tweety ring worn by Erica at all times. A lock of hair was also present at the scene.

With three innocent little girls abducted and murdered in grisly fashions, there was no denying that a serial killer was on the loose in Belize City. The families of Sherilee Nicholas, Jackie Fern Malic, and Erica Wills gathered together along with friends to hold candlelight vigils in order to draw attention to these horrifying crimes. Around 1,000 people attended the vigil. Naturally, parents and other members of the public were outraged and continuously demanded that the police catch the culprit before any more innocent children would fall victim. The police did their best in order to track down all leads and even issued a curfew directed at underaged children.

But it wouldn't prove to be enough as the Belize Ripper struck one final time in the next year.

Noemi Hernandez

The last victim was Noemi Hernandez, who left home to run an errand on Mosul Street on February 15, 2000. She wouldn't be seen again until nine days later, when her body was found near the Belize River. The pattern with Sherilee Nicholas and Jackie Fern Malic was consistent as the 14-year-old Noemi had also received multiple stab wounds to the face and neck. Even more horrifying, many of her body parts had been severed and could not be recovered. She was identified by her father as he recognized the pair of blue jeans she had on from the day she disappeared, though he was so grief-stricken that he kept holding out hope that Noemi would return to him one day.

The Investigation

With the Belize Ripper getting widespread notoriety and comparisons to the infamous Jack the Ripper, the police were under tremendous pressure to get results. The sheer barbarity of the murders had shocked not only the populace of Belize City, but it also became a matter of pride for the national police force. Though small, the Belize Police had built a reputation for its professionalism and cooperation with various international law enforcement agencies. It was through their proactive measures that they were able to curb and even eliminate the marijuana trade. They even stopped several shipments of other drugs such as heroin and cocaine through the Belize coast and jungles.

Thus, they wanted to show the same level of professionalism and efficiency when it came to finding the maniacal serial killer who had started targeting innocent children. They also sought out tips that were thoroughly investigated, but a lot of those tips proved to be redundant as they pointed to people who the police had already checked out. The police also imposed a curfew from 8 p.m. to 6 a.m. for all underaged children—specifically anyone who was 16 or younger—and also stationed guards around school playgrounds.

However, these murders showed that the police were out of their depth when it came to investigating such gruesome crimes. It proved to be frustrating to the police that they weren't able to discover the identity of the serial killer in a country that only has two main highways. Moreover, the public outrage continued to give them a bloody nose, so they turned to the FBI and Scotland Yard for expert assistance. So far, neither agency has confirmed or denied its involvement.

The Desperation of Poverty

The pattern of the victims being picked by the Belize Ripper also brought forward a disturbing facet to this case. The victims hailed from single-parent homes living in relative poverty, with their parents working menial jobs for meager pay. Not only was money tight in such homes, but the parents' time also was, as they would go off to work even before the kids had left for school. Thus, there were rare moments when the parents could spend any time with their children.

Erminda Reid, who taught Sherilee Nicholas in fourth grade, confirmed this. According to her, there were several times when Sherilee would come to school much earlier just so Reid could comb her hair properly, the reason being that Sherilee's mother didn't have enough time to do it as she was always rushing to work.

This fact made Reid even more suspicious when she observed that Sherilee would often be late when returning from recess. Moreover, Sherilee would always have some piece of fruit with her that she had gotten from the carts around the school. This was highly suspect as it was very difficult, if not impossible, for Sherilee to keep buying random pieces of fruit on the low salary that her mother made. Similar observations were made with Jackie Fern Malic. Every now and then, Jackie would go to her grandmother's house with some new clothes and even money. No one had any idea where she got them from, nor did anyone ever ask her.

It wasn't uncommon for young children in Sherilee's situation to be offered money or treats in return for sexual favors and even abuse. This brings up the dark possibility that such poverty-stricken children may actually start getting sexually active. This was confirmed by a private research group called the National Organization for Protection from Child Abuse, and there was the grim possibility that children getting caught in such a vicious cycle may unwittingly be falling into a fatal trap.

The Suspect

Michael Williams

As attributed earlier, 40-year-old mechanic Michael Williams was the only person arrested for the murder of Jackie Fern Malic. This was based on Adelma Malic's statement, where she mentioned that Williams seemed insistent on dropping just her and Jackie at school, even though there were other children going that way. She also claimed that Williams looked "angry and furious," but at the same time, she didn't tell the police that she thought Williams was responsible for Jackie's murder.

Before Jackie's body was discovered, Williams was brought in for questioning and subsequently released. Two days later, Jackie's body was found. When the police questioned more witnesses regarding Williams, they spoke to a 23-year-old woman who claimed Williams molested her when she was a child, which would put Williams in his late 20s. Thus, the police went ahead and arrested him.

Nevertheless, the police had no evidence against the 40-year-old mechanic. In fact, Williams had several customers who claimed to have met him on the day Jackie went missing. This also included a police officer who had seen him at his Belize City auto shop. Moreover, Williams was in custody when Erica Wills went missing in June 1999. Based on this, all the charges against Williams were dropped.

To date, Michael Williams is the only suspect who was arrested for the murders.

The Aftermath

The exploits of the Belize Ripper rocked the foundation of a small Caribbean country, so much so that even after his bloody trail ended, more gruesome and dangerous incidents started taking place. As recently as 2018, three children were almost kidnapped by a Caucasian man in September who had lured them to his white van painted with decorations. His attempts were foiled when the children started hitting him as he tried to force the youngest one into his van. He managed to flee the scene but was later arrested.

In June 2012, 13-year-old Jasmine Lowe disappeared after leaving her house in the Cayo District to join the Girl Scouts at a Diamond Jubilee celebration in Belmopan. Her mother claimed that she was headed to a salon before making her way to the event. She was found dead a couple of days later, and her decomposing body had been dumped near a farm. Witnesses say that she was seen getting into a white taxi at around 2 p.m. after she left her house. Days after Lowe's corpse was found, approximately 13 children informed the police that they had also been lured into a white taxi when the driver promised them money. The police were led to a suspect, and they searched his vehicle. A ring belonging to Jasmine Lowe and some of her hair was found in the car. The 33-year-old man was then arrested and sentenced to 10 years in 2017; however, this was for aggravated sexual assault against another 16-year-old girl. He is still waiting to be tried for murdering Jasmine Lowe.

In August 2010, two children went missing from Cattle Landing, Toledo District, where they were selling limes and craboo. They had gone with their father by bus, and their father had let them board another bus with their uncle so that they could get to Cattle Landing. They were last seen by their uncle at around 10 a.m. with their buckets and by others at about 4 in the afternoon. They were never found. Rumor has it that they were kidnapped by the owner of a nearby crocodile sanctuary who fed them to its inhabitants.

Such incidents and more have gone on to prove that the children of Belize are not safe and can become easy prey for all kinds of murderous psychopaths such as the Belize Ripper. While the police are working as hard as possible to ensure a sense of security, a significant chunk of the responsibility falls on the parents as well as the children to look out for any suspicious characters in their neighborhoods who try to entice them with promises of money and other presents. Still, the parents of the Belize Ripper's victims continue to grieve over the tragic and untimely loss of their children and the lack of progress by the police to bring the killer to justice. The police have offered a reward of $100,000 for any information that could lead to an arrest; however, parents such as June Gabourel feel that the case has gone cold along with any trail of the Belize Ripper.

THE ŁÓDŹ GAY MURDERS

The problem with forbidden love is that it can lead to acts of desperation. In a religiously conservative country like Poland, where there have been laws that facilitate LGBTQ people in place since the 1930s, the fact remains that the populace has some of the worst views regarding LGBTQ rights around the world. The queer community is not amply protected against hate speech and hate crime. In the backdrop of such an environment, one major Polish city saw a bloody rampage where seven men were brutally killed, almost all of them in the comfort of their own homes, in the twilight of the 20th century. Their only crime: They were gay men seeking love.

The Method

Between 1988 and 1993, the Łódź gay community lost seven men as they were in the comfort of their own homes and entertaining young lovers. The killer would meet his victims at places frequented by gay men, such as the Fabryczna station, and then accompany them to their homes, where they would engage in sexual activities. All of the victims were stabbed, but the killer would always pick a knife from the victim's own house. While most died due to blood loss, other times, the victims were killed by asphyxiation or blunt-force trauma. The killer would then steal any valuables he could find from the house, such as electronics, cash, and jewelry.

The Victims

The names of the victims have been altered to protect the identities of their families.

Stefan W.

The first known victim was 37-year-old Stefan W., who was found dead in his Grabowa Street Apartment on September 27, 1988. One of the neighbors reported to the police a foul stench coming from the apartment. The neighbor also said that the resident, Stefan W., was used to having strange men over and partying through the night, inferring that Stefan W. was homosexual. She also said that she hadn't seen her neighbor for over ten days. Once the police and firefighters broke into the apartment, they were instantly taken aback by the foul odor of Stefan W.'s decaying corpse and gas leaking from the stove. He was found lying on a couch with bedding placed on him that had been bloodied. His legs were tied up with electrical wire, and then he was hogtied by his left arm. He had been stabbed to death with a kitchen knife multiple times, six in the back and chest, which also pierced his heart. A heavy bookcase had also been thrown over him.

The murder weapon was found near the couch at the scene, and it also had fingerprints. Additionally, there were items missing from the house, such as electronics and various other valuables. The closets had been emptied, and clothes were strewn around everywhere. The killer had stolen some expensive equipment such as a VCR, camera, a wedding ring, gold signets, a leather coat, a radio, some videotapes, and even a photo album. The killer also took cash as well as the apartment keys. This was all corroborated by the victim's family.

It emerged during the course of the investigation that Stefan W. was, in fact, a homosexual man as insinuated by his neighbor, and was last seen on September 19, 1988, at an establishment frequented by many gay men called the Łódź 'pickets' in the Łódź Fabryczna station. He used to meet several like-minded people there, including artists, academics, as well as men who offered sexual services to other homosexual men. These were known as 'zulas.' Stefan was known among the gay community for being wealthy and for hosting exciting parties, and he did not hesitate to boast about it.

It is possible that Stefan W. may have met his killer, who was posing as a gay man at the 'pickets,' and then invited him over to his place. The stranger might have known about Stefan W.'s wealth and heady lifestyle and decided to target him. According to the police, there are chances of the murder either being due to a lover's quarrel or being entirely premeditated to commit the robbery. Based on the neighbors' testimonies, the victim had brought his killer to the apartment at around 7 p.m., and they all heard strange noises from his apartment, including moaning and the moving of furniture. One witness saw a young man flee the apartment via the stairs. The man was described as around 30 years old with short blond hair, a round face, and a stocky build. He appeared to be about 5'7". But so far, no suspect has emerged.

Jacek C.

The next victim was 40-year-old Jacek C., who was found dead in his Ernst Thalmann Street apartment on August 4, 1989. He was reported missing when he did not come into work after being last seen on July 30 of that same year. He worked as a tour organizer for a travel agency and had a sterling reputation for never being tardy. When he did not pick up his phone on August 3, his colleagues headed to his apartment and found the door locked. They spoke to a neighbor and agreed that it was uncharacteristic of Jacek simply to disappear without informing anyone. They decided that they would call the police the next day. When the police arrived, the neighbor complained about a strange odor coming from the apartment and also gave them a set of keys she found in the stairwell earlier. The keys led into Jacek C.'s apartment.

Jacek C. was found inside, lying dead on the couch, wearing a T-shirt and underwear. His hands were tied with string, and around his neck was a noose. His legs had been tied up with his trouser belt. His apartment had also been ransacked as Stefan W.'s had been. Cash and a large TV had been stolen from the house. However, Jacek was murdered by suffocation as the killer stuffed a kitchen dishcloth in his mouth.

Jacek C. was last seen on July 30, 1989, when he visited his mother and had left her home at around 4:30 p.m. He had told her that he was expecting company and had to go. He lived alone and was, in fact, homosexual, just like Stefan W. was. However, he kept it a secret from family as well as his work colleagues for fear of exposure and humiliation. He was not known to frequent common meeting places for gay men, such as the Łódź pickets, and he was not in a permanent relationship.

The police have once again theorized that this could also be a robbery-turned-murder, or it may have been a crime of passion. Jacek himself had once reported such a robbery by a man to the police, which led them to believe that his murder might be in retaliation for it. Despite them questioning over 60 people, the police are nowhere close to identifying a suspect.

Bogdan J.

A few months later, the body of 50-year-old Bogdan J. was discovered in his apartment on Łanowa Street on November 23, 1989. The killer had stabbed him with a knife while having sex. An actor by trade, he was last seen on November 21, 1989. When he hadn't shown up to work for several days, his friends started calling him but got no response. They then informed his mother, who went along with her daughter to his apartment. The apartment was not properly locked, and they were quickly able to enter the horrible and shocking scene that awaited them. Bogdan J.'s partially naked body was lying on the couch, with a bloodied bed sheet underneath him. Based on the examination, the killer had used great force to stab the victim, and it appeared the victim had tried to defend himself, which resulted in several bruises and defensive wounds.

The pattern established by the previous murders continued. A kitchen knife covered in blood was found in one of the rooms, and several items were stolen, such as a VCR, gold jewelry, a signet ring, a pair of binoculars, a watch, and other items of clothing.

Unlike Jacek, Bogdan was very open and flamboyant about his sexuality and was a regular feature at the Łódź pickets. He was also very carefree about the people he spent time with and would bring anyone home right after the first meeting. He had been seeing a young student at one point, but they broke it off as he was promiscuous and unwilling to settle down.

Bogdan J. was last seen on November 21, 1989, with a friend at a party; they left at around 11 p.m. According to the friend, they went to the bus stop together, where Bogdan J. spotted a young man waiting for a tram. Bogdan then told his friend he would go and try his luck, and sure enough, the two started chatting and headed for a taxicab.

Later, when the friend arrived home, he tried contacting Bogdan at home. The call was picked up and then hung up quickly. The friend assumed that they needed privacy, so he did not call again. He described this young man as medium build with blond hair with highlights. He looked like he was in his early 20s and was wearing a denim jacket, wide trousers, and white leather shoes with black tops. The blond hair matched the description of the person seen leaving Stefan W.'s apartment. However, no viable suspect could be identified.

Andrzej S.

Forty-one-year-old Andrzej S. was the next to be killed as his body was found in his Gładka Street apartment on March 5, 1990. The cause of death was stabbing by knife, similar to previous victims. His body had several stab wounds that had been struck with brute force aimed at the neck, chest, back, and head. Once again, a kitchen knife was used to commit the murder, and there was an unfolded couch with bloodied sheets spread over them. Following the established pattern, the killer then burgled the house, but all he managed to steal was a TV, some clothes, and money.

Unlike some of the previous victims, Andrzej S. was a disability pensioner with limited means. Nevertheless, he also frequented the Łódź pickets and often boasted about having a wealthy family abroad, possibly to attract more men to him. He also wasn't shy about inviting other men to his place and was last seen on February 25, 1990.

This time, there was one slight oddity. Though the killer upended the whole place looking for valuables, he did not make off with a secret notebook belonging to Andrzej S. It contained over 200 names and phone numbers of his friends and lovers. This provided the police with a targeted cluster to question; nevertheless, they were not able to find the killer.

Jakub M.

The fifth homosexual man to fall victim was another 41-year-old man named Jakub M. Unlike the previous victims, his body was found in a forest in Głowno on the same day he was murdered, July 31, 1990. The body was placed near an abandoned Volkswagen Beetle and was almost entirely nude. His clothes had been neatly folded next to the car, and a wallet full of money and a watch were also found in the pile. The cause of death was strangulation.

Jakub M. had started living in a separate portion of his parent's house near Łódź, which also had a private entrance. Jakub M. used this entrance to bring in guests for his alcohol-focused soirees. He also frequented the gay dating scene at a bar at the Łódź Fabryczny Station, where he had been last seen that afternoon. However, he did not advertise a great deal about his sexuality. He preferred chatting up younger men, but witnesses say that he wasn't very lucky with them, primarily due to his excessive alcoholism. It wasn't rare for him to get drunk and then robbed and beat up by the men he would pick up, and in fact, witnesses claim to have seen him drinking a glass of vodka before driving away. According to his mother, there was a car parked outside the house that night, and there were sounds of a party happening. It was very likely that the killer must have been one of them. It appears that Jakub M. was killed while driving his guest back to town or that the killer was cautious about Jakub's parents hearing them, which is why he took him to a secluded spot like the forest. Nothing was stolen from Jakub M.'s dwelling.

Jan D.

Seven months later, the body of 48-year-old Jan D. was found in a room on top of his restaurant building in Łagiewniki on February 20, 1992, the same day he was killed. His body was found by a tenant who was renting a room from him. His naked body was lying on the carpet and covered with a duvet and pillow. An electrical wire was coiled around his neck, and the room itself was covered in black soot because of a chair that had caught fire from a stove. The cause of death was a vicious blow to the head, and the body had other injuries such as a broken nose.

Jan D. was a restaurant proprietor, and his small establishment also had rooms upstairs from which he supplemented his income by renting them out. He had moved from Wrocław to Łódź a few years before and did not visit the pickets. Instead, he had a tendency to hire attractive young men at his restaurant who he could then coerce into sexual favors for promotions and other benefits. Most of them would leave due to such advances. He also used personal ads in newspapers to find more liaisons.

During the investigation, it emerged that Jan had sold the establishment off for a considerable sum of money which he then put in a bank. The killer may have caught wind of this and assumed that the money was in his house. No suspects could be found.

Kazimierz K.

The last known victim was retired 62-year-old pensioner Kazimierz K. who was killed on July 11, 1993. His body was discovered on July 12, 1993, in his Konstytucyjna Street apartment. Kazimierz was actually quite popular among the Łódź gay community and would either find men at the Łódź Fabryczna station or would have others bring partners to him. At one of these get-togethers on July 10, 1993, he had a few men over at his apartment, and someone he knew brought him a young man named Roman.

They hit it off, and his friend left, leaving Roman with Kazimierz K. Everyone else then began to depart, knowing that Roman was going to stay behind. When his friends tried contacting him the next day, they ended up going to his place after getting no answer. The door was unlocked, and they went inside to find Kazimierz K. dead on his couch with sheets underneath him. He was dressed in a bathrobe and had been heavily injured on the head and face. He had been asphyxiated to death as per the autopsy.

When the police questioned the friend who had brought Roman along, he told them that he had met Roman a couple of days before at the Dąbrowski Square pickets and had apparently had sexual liaisons with him before bringing him to Kazimierz K. He also mentioned that the night they were heading to Kazimierz's place, they took the bus with another friend who asked Roman about himself. But Roman's answers were carefully selected and thought out as if he was trying to conceal something.

As there were several witnesses who had seen Roman, the police were finally able to get a composite sketch. He was described as about 27 years old, 5'7", with a medium build and hazel eyes. He also had some dots tattooed near his left eye and neck, as well as some on his left-hand fingers. He dressed modestly and also smoked. He was nervous around some of the female guests at Kazimierz K.'s party, and one woman mentioned that he did not let her kiss him.

The Investigation

Aside from the fact that the killer could not be located within the areas frequented by the gay community, one of the primary reasons why the police never made much progress in catching the killer was due to the secrecy within the gay community itself. Public opinion about homosexuality in a country like Poland, with an over 80% Roman Catholic population, made gay men and women very wary about revealing their sexuality openly in the 1980s and 1990s for fear of embarrassment, humiliation, and revulsion from friends and family, not to mention hate crimes.

Most gay men and women would be beaten up or robbed by other people whom they had picked up. Hence, this is why many of them preferred to keep any incidents such as robberies, assaults, and other altercations to themselves instead of going to the police, as it would mean revealing what they were doing with those people in the first place. But when the murders started happening with greater regularity, the gay community of Łódź began cooperating with the authorities.

Contrary to the perceptions in the gay community about any prejudicial attitudes by the police, they actually considered the murders to be one of their highest priorities. They were, however, hindered by the fact that it took a while before the gay community started cooperating with them, which may have given the killer enough time to get bolder and better at covering his tracks.

The police were able to question roughly 400 people, including other gay men, witnesses at gay-friendly establishments frequently visited by the victims, friends and family members, and also former lovers. They also went door-to-door at the last known sightings of Roman, as per Kazimierz K.'s friend, and they also checked any correctional facilities to see if he had a prior criminal record. The composite sketch of Roman based on eyewitness accounts was circulated among the local and national press, but the police could not find any further leads.

There were a few other murders of homosexual men in Łódź after Kazimierz K.'s killing. Still, they did not appear to be related to the earlier seven murders as the latter killers were caught, but none of them took responsibility for the previous seven. Therefore, the killer appeared to have stopped or moved away right after Kazimierz K., and if it is indeed Roman, there is no trace of him.

The friend of Kazimierz K., who had introduced Roman to him, testified that Roman had divulged a lot about himself. According to him, Roman lived on Rzgowska Street and worked in a cotton factory. When he was 15, Roman had been molested by a teacher. But those leads did not yield any fruit for the investigation. The friend of Kazimierz K. eventually died of AIDS.

Thus the mystery of the Łódź Gay Murders remains unsolved to this day.

10

THE FAMILY MURDERS

It only takes one serial killer to wreak havoc. It takes more than one working in tandem to have people bolting their doors. But no one could have imagined the level of organization that could be achieved by an entire family. This wasn't a 'family' in the traditional sense that got together on special occasions or went on picnics over the weekends. This was a different kind of family: a violent, brutal, sadistic, and utterly unhinged family that preyed upon innocent young men as if it were the law of the jungle.

This is the story of the most gruesome murders committed in ways that stretch the limits of barbarity throughout history. This is the story of a group of people so remorseless, so depraved, that they saw nothing sacred as they held their victims captive and took sick pleasure in ripping them apart, quite literally. This is the story of "The Family," a group of around 30 men and women, including some of Australia's high society, who were responsible for about 150 cases of rape, as well as abductions, druggings, mutilations, and five murders by sodomizing their victims to death.

The Method

The most important aspect of The Family's success was being able to lure their victims to them in order to abduct them. To ensure this, the ringleader of The Family developed a network of like-minded people whose lifestyle was all about sexual sadism. Their main target was young boys, whether they were homosexual or not, and the younger, the better. Their youngest-known murder victim was 14 years old.

The ringleader often used enablers such as male prostitutes, cross-dressers, transgender people, and so on to lure young boys to them. They acted as helpers who brought the unsuspecting victims into their car, drugged, abducted, and then transported them. They also participated in the gruesome sexual violence with the ringleader, kept the victims captive till they were dead, assisted in the mutilation of the victims, and dumped the bodies at an indiscreet location. Above all else, they kept total silence about their activities and never implicated each other, including the ringleader of the entire operation.

They would entice young men with invitations to exclusive parties and offer them free drinks and women. Once the boys accepted the offer, the enablers would give them a beverage containing a sedative such as Rohypnol or Mandrax. Other times, the ringleader would seek out hitchhikers on the wide-open roads of Adelaide. Another ploy was to ask a young boy to help him with car troubles after he had pulled out the vehicle's choke or unscrewed his car muffler, which would give him enough opportunity to drug the unsuspecting youth and stash them in his car.

The moniker of "The Family" was unwittingly given to them after a police interview where a detective boldly claimed that they would "break up the happy family" since this particular 'family' had a diabolical way of being happy.

The Victims

The Family was responsible for the abduction of 150 young men and women who were kidnapped, drugged, and raped. Five victims that came to be known as "The Family Murders" included young boys and men from the ages of 14 to 25 who were found dead with severely mutilated bodies. They had been murdered horrendously with their last moments an agonizing hell as the killers thrust blunt objects through their anus till the lining inside split, causing anal bleeding until they died. They were kept alive for as little as 24 hours to as much as five weeks, during which time they were subjected to brutal physical torture and sadism that involved mutilations, hackings, using surgery to commit torture, and so on. The victims were also found with all sorts of drugs and sedatives in their system, most likely used during the abductions and to keep victims alive while being tortured.

Alan Barnes

Sixteen-year-old Alan Arthur Barnes went missing on June 17, 1979, after having spent the night in Cheltenham at Darko Kastelan's house. They were both planning to hitchhike to Barnes's house in Salisbury as it happened to be a Sunday. They were dropped off at a bus stop near Grand Junction Road by Kastelan's brother, and Darko himself returned home shortly after. Barnes was last seen by a witness getting into a white Holden HQ sedan near Production Road.

Seven days later, his body was found near the South Para reservoir underneath a bridge on June 24, 1979. The autopsy revealed that he had been viciously tortured and sexually assaulted and was likely killed on June 22 or 23, 1979, after being subjected to torture and rape for several days. He also appeared to have alcohol and a sedative in his blood. Interestingly, his body seemed to have been cleaned and dressed again in his own clothes before it was dumped. The cause of death was severe blood loss from massive anal injuries.

Barnes was working with vending machines a few days a week prior to his death and had recently become friends with Darko Kastelan. Though he was living with his family in Salisbury, he would often spend the weekends in Cheltenham. According to the people who knew him, Barnes was in no way homosexual and, in fact, had been charged by the police before for raping a female victim. However, the complaint never made it to court as it appeared the incident was actually consensual.

Neil Muir

Two months later, 25-year-old Neil Frederick Muir went missing on August 27, 1979, from Hindley Street in Adelaide. His severely mutilated body was found near the Port Adelaide River at a place called Mutton Cove the next day on August 28, 1979. The killer had cut his body into four parts, at the neck, above the hips, and just above the knees, and then packed it in garbage bags before throwing it off the jetty at Mutton Cove. Furthermore, his organs were removed, his scrotum was cut open, and his testicles were removed. The penis shaft itself was ripped open down the midline, and its head was chopped off. His hands and fingers had also been twisted, and curiously, the skin with tattoos on it had been removed and was found along with the remains.

The cause of death appears to be blood loss due to anal injuries, just like Alan Barnes. Muir was a known heroin addict, but a toxicology report could not be furnished because of the missing internal organs. The police suspected that Muir was a male prostitute, and he would often visit places where gay men met. Muir was last seen with a man named Dr. Millhouse at around 3 p.m. the day he went missing. It was speculated that Dr. Millhouse provided Muir with drugs in exchange for sexual favors, but he was acquitted when the case went to trial.

Following his release, Dr. Millhouse moved out of Adelaide. But there were more gruesome murders to come.

Peter Stogneff

It would be two years until the next victim emerged. At age 14, Peter Stogneff was the youngest victim of The Family murders. The night before his disappearance, he and his uncle—who happened to be the same age as him—were planning to skip school and meet at the Rundle Mall. However, the plan was canceled, but Stogneff still missed school regardless on August 27, 1981. He was seen by a witness at Tea Tree Plaza with someone who appeared to be a transvestite. Stogneff never returned home after that.

His body was found ten months later at the side of the road at Two Wells near Middle Beach, around 30 miles away from Adelaide, on June 23, 1982. It had been unwittingly set on fire as part of a farmer's land burning. It was only noticed when they removed a bush, but by then, the body had burnt to a skeleton. Thus the cause of death could not be determined, nor could the authorities check the body for toxicity. The body was also hacked into four different portions, just like that of Neil Muir. It is also unclear whether or not the organs were removed.

Mark Langley

Between Stogneff's disappearance and discovery, 18-year-old Mark Langley was the fourth person to go missing on February 27, 1982. A resident of Newton, he was attending a party in Windsor Gardens but was seen departing along with a male and female. From there, they headed to the War Memorial Drive by car. At some point, Langley had an argument with the male acquaintance, after which he got out of the car and walked away. While the male and female acquaintances drove away, they came back to pick him up a few minutes later. But by then, Langley had disappeared.

His body wouldn't be found until over a week later when it was discovered in some scrubs at Sprigg Road in Piccadilly. From the examination, it appears that Langley had been killed on the night that he disappeared and had been dumped immediately afterward. The cause of death was blood loss due to anal injuries, just like Barnes and Muir. His body had also been severely mutilated, including a cut from his navel to the pubic area. The hair around the area had been shaved, and a portion of his small intestine had been removed. He also had been given a sedative as per the toxicology reports. However, the body was not hacked into different portions like in the case of Muir and Stogneff. In fact, he was washed and dressed again in his own clothes, just like Barnes.

Richard Kelvin

The following year, 15-year-old Richard Kelvin was walking his friend to a bus stop on O'Connell Street in North Adelaide at around 6 p.m. on June 5, 1983. He was supposed to call his girlfriend from a payphone and then head straight home to Ward Street in North Adelaide to have dinner. It was a Sunday, and he had school the next day, but Kelvin never made it home. According to an eyewitness, there was an argument between male and female voices which resulted in shouting, followed by the sound of a car driving away at full speed. It was prominent as it had a loud muffler. Right after that, Kelvin vanished.

His body was found near Kersbrook on Airstrip Road in some bushes next to an airfield on July 24, 1983. It appeared to have been there for days, possibly since July 10 or 11. The autopsy suggests that Kelvin had been killed on July 10, 1983, which means he had been kept alive for five whole weeks to suffer. The cause of death is consistent with that of Barnes, Muir, and Langley, as Kelvin was also killed due to severe blood loss from persistent anal injuries. It also appeared that he had been subjected to a large blunt object thrust into his rectum. He was also heavily drugged with various sedatives such as Rohypnol, Valium, Amatel, Noctec, and Mandrax, and he had been given a haircut while he was held prisoner. His body had also been washed and dressed up again in his clothes before it was dumped.

The Investigation

As the police could find no link between the five young men, the various locations that they were abducted from, or the witness accounts of the people they were last seen with, the only other lead they had was the type of drugs in the victims' bloodstreams when they were found. In the case of Mark Langley and Richard Kelvin, they had a regulated sedative called Mandrax in their system, which had limited stock in Australia since 1978. The police were able to find a prescription for Mandrax made out to "B. von Einem."

This struck them as a promising lead as Bevan Spencer von Einem had been accused of previously sexually assaulting a young man. He was also present at the location where two homosexual men named Dr. George Duncan and Robert James were thrown into a river on May 10, 1972. Duncan drowned at the scene, but von Einem was able to rescue James and take him to a hospital. The spot from where Duncan and James were thrown off happened to be a secret meeting place for homosexuals, considering that homosexual relations were still illegal until 1975. Von Einem claims he was driving in the area by happenstance.

He was questioned at his residence in northern Adelaide four days after the discovery of Richard Kelvin's brutalized corpse. Von Einem's demeanor felt odd to the police, as he initially refused to answer any questions without his lawyer present. He then claimed that he had never seen Kelvin and that he was bedridden with flu on the night of Kelvin's abduction and was off from work for the subsequent week. Curiously, he outrightly said that he would never do any of the crimes that were committed against Kelvin as he found them to be unethical, which the police found a strange thing to say.

Nevertheless, the police were able to locate a bottle of Mandrax at his house, which von Einem claimed was used to help him with a sleep disorder. He also had a bottle of Noctec which was carefully hidden behind a closet, another drug found in Richard Kelvin's bloodstream. When the police inquired about the Noctec, von Einem became evasive and claimed that he rarely used it. The police also took some hair and blood samples for testing along with some carpets from his house at von Einem's consent. The police had gotten enough signals from von Einem's behavior and answers, as well as the bottles of drugs, to identify him as the prime suspect.

During forensic analysis, several fibers from Kelvin's clothing and his hair were found on the carpet taken from von Einem's house. This confirmed that Kelvin was at von Einem's home, despite von Einem's claim that he didn't even know him. There were also other fibers found on Kelvin's clothes which turned out to come from a cardigan belonging to von Einem, which suggested that the two had direct physical contact.

Later, the police also came into contact with a man simply known as "Mr. B," who told them all about von Einem's proclivities and methods. Mr. B claimed von Einem trapped young men, such as hitchhikers and potential drug addicts, aside from unsuspecting teenagers and abducted them after giving them drugged beverages. According to Mr. B, von Einem then took those young men to his previous residence in Campbelltown, where he raped and tortured them. However, they would be released the next day.

According to Mr. B., von Einem was also responsible for the abduction and murder of Alan Barnes, and the police were able to corroborate the injuries inflicted on Barnes with those on Kelvin. He claimed that Barnes used to work refilling vending machines, and he would frequently visit a company on his route where von Einem was working as an accountant. Mr. B. also claimed in his testimony that he was in the white Holden sedan with von Einem, which was used to abduct Barnes.

Mr. B. then shocked the police with details of von Einem's associates and how they helped him to abduct young men by drugging them and then participated in von Einem's own brand of sexually sadistic torture and violent murder. He provided details of the members of von Einem's network but also claimed that he himself was in no way responsible for any of the murders. The police then started questioning those associates provided by Mr. B. and also raided several locations connected to them and to von Einem. They were unable to get much information or clues out of them; however, the police had enough to build a case against von Einem and evidence which placed Richard Kelvin at von Einem's house at the time of the murder.

He was subsequently arrested on November 3, 1983, and charged with murdering Richard Kelvin. By February 1984, von Einem was faced with the grim possibility of a trial, which is when he changed his statement that he had, in fact, met Kelvin on the night he was killed. He spun a tale about how he almost ran over Kelvin while he was trying to park his car and, while talking to him, felt that Kelvin may be bisexual. He then stated that the two had a candid conversation about problems Kelvin was having at school, after which Kelvin accompanied von Einem to his house willingly, where he stayed for two hours. Von Einem then stated that he had entertained Kelvin in his bedroom by playing a large gold harp, which explained how his clothing fibers had ended up on the carpet. As for the threads from von Einem's cardigan, he claimed that it was when they had had a heart-to-heart embrace when Kelvin seemingly opened up about being bullied at school. Finally, von Einem stated that he dropped Kelvin off near the Royal Adelaide Hospital and even gave him money for a cab.

The new statement from von Einem was far too outlandish, as it was flawed. For one thing, it was unlikely for a 15-year-old to implicitly trust someone he had just met so much so that he would go to his house willingly and speak openly. Second of all, Kelvin already had a girlfriend, which suggested that he was pretty sure of his sexual inclinations. And finally, this new statement was in total contradiction to von Einem's first one, claiming that he was bedridden with the flu. This, coupled with the mounting evidence of the direct physical contact between von Einem and Kelvin, was enough for the magistrate to order von Einem to be tried for Kelvin's murder.

Ultimately, von Einem was found guilty on November 5, 1984, for the murder of Richard Kelvin. According to Australian law, he was automatically awarded a life sentence with an additional punishment of a 24-year non-parole period. To this day, he remains in a maximum-security wing of Port Augusta prison since 2007, though he was previously incarcerated at Yatala Labour

Prison. Though it was possible for him to seek parole in the late 2000s, new legislation spearheaded by Mike Rann, the premier of South Australia at the time, ensured that Einem's parole privileges would be revoked. He was caught concealing child pornography in his cell in 2008, for which he pled guilty. He was also accused of raping a fellow inmate in Yatala Prison in 2007.

CONCLUSION

Within these four frightening volumes, one thing is absolutely clear: There is no end to the brutality and callousness of people. Whether for unholy sexual sadism or the desire to prey upon the most vulnerable of society, every country, every town, and every neighborhood has the possibility of a serial killer hiding in their midst, waiting for something to snap so that they begin bringing their nightmarish fantasies to life. Most will go unheard of, but not if we all keep our eyes and ears peeled to the dangers lurking in the shadows, waiting for us at every turn. This will ensure that what happened to the men, women, and children in these pages won't happen to any of us.

And never forget that there are far more crimes the world can't even begin to imagine. The next series by

D.R. Werner, titled *Unsolved True Crime: 10 Frightening Cases of Mystery, Murder, and Mayhem,* will take you on a brand-new journey full of excitement, thrills, mystery, and lawlessness that has baffled the finest minds of law enforcement to date.

Until the next time...

MORE FROM D.R. WERNER

Search D.R. Werner on Amazon
AND
Visit www.DRWernerbooks.com

You can also join the Facebook group @
https://www.facebook.com/groups/drwernerbooks

REFERENCES

ABC News. (2010, December 14). *Are Atlantic City murders tied to N.Y. serial killer?* ABC News. https://abcnews.go.com/TheLaw/bodies-long-island-beach-serial-killer-loose/story?id=12399090

Amandala Newspaper. (2018, October 6). *Revisiting past child abductions in Belize and missing children.* Amandala Newspaper. https://amandala.com.bz/news/revisiting-child-abductions-belize-missing-children/

Cleveland Police Museum. (2016). *Torso murders - Cleveland Police Museum.* Cleveland Police Museum. https://www.clevelandpolicemuseum.org/collections/torso-murders/

Colonial Parkway murders: Report - Colonial ghosts. (2020, February 28). ColonialGhosts.com. https://colonial

ghosts.com/the-colonial-parkway-murders-a-report/

Combs, B. (2011, February 6). *Victims of the eastbound strangler*. Serial Killers Podcast. http://serialkillers.briancombs.net/3027/victims-of-the-eastbound-strangler/

Corbin, C. (2015, March 25). *Atlantic City authorities eye "more than one" person of interest in 2006 unsolved prostitute murders*. Fox News. https://www.foxnews.com/us/atlantic-city-authorities-eye-more-than-one-person-of-interest-in-2006-unsolved-prostitute-murders

Crime Investigation Australia (Series 1 Episode 16). (n.d.). Crime & Investigation Network.

Criminal Minds Wiki. (2019). *The Mad Butcher of Kingsbury Run*. Criminal Minds Wiki. https://criminalminds.fandom.com/wiki/The_Mad_Butcher_of_Kingsbury_Run

Darling, J. (1999, September 22). *Column one: Serial killer is stalking the oasis : Seven girls have been slain in tiny Belize in the past year. The crimes underscore growing dysfunction in the former British colony*. Los Angeles Times. https://www.latimes.com/archives/la-xpm-1999-sep-22-mn-12880-story.html

Daugherty, K. (2021, September 27). *Retired police officer who worked Oakland County Child Killer cold case highlighted in book*. Livingston Daily Press & Argus. https://

www.livingstondaily.com/story/news/local/2021/09/27/oakland-county-child-killer-brighton-retired-officers-work-highlighted-book-the-snow-killings/8419465002/

Davan-Soulas, M. (2016, March 4). Retour sur les affaires des "Disparus de l'Isère" - Société - MYTF1News. Web.archive.org. https://web.archive.org/web/20160304000849/http://lci.tf1.fr/france/faits-divers/retour-sur-les-affaires-des-disparus-de-l-isere-8191091.html

DeMarco, L., & Dealer, T. P. (2018, October 12). *Cleveland's infamous Torso Murders: 80 years later, the fascination endures (vintage photos)*. Cleveland. https://www.cleveland.com/life-and-culture/erry-2018/10/55d2b5ea596983/clevelands-infamous-torso-murd.html

DNA links new suspect to 1970's Oakland County Child Killings. (2011, May 19). CBS Detroit. https://detroit.cbslocal.com/2011/05/19/dna-links-new-suspect-to-1970s-oakland-county-child-killings/

Giacomazzo, B. (2021, December 28). *How "the monster with 21 faces" poisoned Japan's candy supply, taunted police, and never got caught*. All That's Interesting. https://allthatsinteresting.com/monster-with-21-faces

Guerrieri, V. (2020, September 29). *The Cleveland Torso Murderer: The scariest serial killer you've never heard of.* Www.mentalfloss.com. https://www.mentalfloss.com/article/632096/cleveland-torso-murderer-unsolved-serial-killer

Haberman, C. (1985, December 10). *Japanese puzzle: The vending machine murders.* The New York Times. http://www.nytimes.com/1985/12/10/world/japanese-puzzle-the-vending-machine-murders.html

Head of School, & admin.slll@anu.edu.au. (n.d.). *Australian place nicknames search.* ANU School of Literature, Languages and Linguistics. https://slll.cass.anu.edu.au/centres/andc/nicknames

Heusner, K. (1999, July 28). *String of murder-rapes hits Belize.* AP NEWS. https://apnews.com/article/c8aa67938a024d74e7a0a8e2ee76ef40

Holter, E., & Adcox, A. (2021, October 22). *35 years later, victims' families in Colonial Parkway Murders still searching for answers, hope DNA advances will solve case.* Dailypress.com/Virginiagazette. https://www.dailypress.com/virginiagazette/va-vg-colonial-parkway-murders-anniversary-1024-20211022-76jkpte6qvez7onybmhbhp7nfi-story.html

IOL. (2007, July 12). *Body-parts find sparks hope in murder case.* Www.iol.co.za. https://www.iol.co.za/

news/africa/body-parts-find-sparks-hope-in-murder-case-361726

Isaacs, D. (2007, September 21). *Man claims to be B1 Butcher*. The Namibian. https://www.namibian.com.na/39798/archive-read/Man-claims-to-be-B1-Butcher-A-50-year-old-man

James Jessen Badal. (2014). *In the wake of the butcher : Cleveland's torso murders*. Kent State University Press.

Les disparues de l'Isère - La cellule d'enquête "Mineurs 38" va bientôt livrer ses conclusions. (2012). France Soir.fr. http://archive.francesoir.fr/actualite/societe/disparues-l-isere-cellule-d%25E2%2580%2599enquete-%25C2%25AB-mineurs-38-%25C2%25BB-va-bientot-livrer-ses-conclusions-48319.html

Lohr, D. (2011, September 6). *Controversial figure in Colonial Parkway murders arrested*. HuffPost. https://www.huffpost.com/entry/fred-atwell-colonial-parkway-murders-arrest_n_947121

MacGowan, D. (2015, January 7). *Monster with 21 faces*. Historic Mysteries. https://www.historicmysteries.com/monster-21-faces/

Medicine Plus. (n.d.). *Paraquat poisoning: MedlinePlus Medical Encyclopedia*. Medlineplus.gov. https://medlineplus.gov/ency/article/001085.htm

Menges, W. (2007a, June 22). *"B1 butcher" still at large*. The Namibian. https://www.namibian.com.na/34794/archive-read/B1-butcher-still-at-large-THE-fifth-day-of-a

Menges, W. (2007b, August 3). *Police mum on B1 Butcher case*. The Namibian. https://www.namibian.com.na/30256/archive-read/Police-mum-on-B1-Butcher-case-THREE-weeks-and

Murderpedia. (n.d.). *Bevan Von Einem | Murderpedia, the encyclopedia of murderers*. Murderpedia.org. https://murderpedia.org/male.V/v/von-einem-bevan.htm

Neuf enfants ont disparu en Isère depuis 1983. (2013, July 25). Franceinfo. https://www.francetvinfo.fr/faits-divers/neuf-enfants-ont-disparu-en-isere-depuis-1983_1662675.html

News 5 Belize. (n.d.). *Revisiting greatest unsolved murder mystery – "Belizean Jack the Ripper"* News 5 Belize. Retrieved April 21, 2022, from https://edition.channel5belize.com/archives/140152

Newton, M. (2010). *The encyclopedia of unsolved crimes / monograph*. Checkmark Books.

Okabe, M. (1985, November 27). *Japanese warned against poisoned soft drinks*. UPI. https://www.upi.com/

Archives/1985/09/27/Japanese-warned-against-poisoned-soft-drinks/9882496641600/

Pavan, B., & Jolly, P. (2013, July 26). *En Isère, le double meurtre de Sarah et Saïda résolu vingt ans après les faits*. Le Monde.fr. https://www.lemonde.fr/societe/article/2013/07/26/en-isere-le-double-meurtre-de-sarah-et-saida-resolu-vingt-ans-plus-tard_3454025_3224.html

Randal Cohen. (2021, August 26). *The Paraquat vending machine murders*. Nadrich & Cohen Accident Injury Lawyers. https://personalinjurylawcal.com/blog/the-paraquat-vending-machine-murders/

Sheets, M. (2021, February 23). *New film links Gilgo Beach serial killings with Atlantic City murders*. Mail Online. https://www.dailymail.co.uk/news/article-9290843/Lifetime-film-connects-Gilgo-Beach-serial-killings-Atlantic-City-murders.html

Sprawa z "Archiwum X" - zabójca z pikiety. (2008, April 30). Onet Wiadomości. https://wiadomosci.onet.pl/kiosk/sprawa-z-archiwum-x-zabojca-z-pikiety/l6v4m

TF1 News. (2016, February 23). *Disparus de l'Isère : trois dossiers relancés - Société - MYTF1News*. Web.archive.org. https://web.archive.org/web/20160223133811/http://lci.tf1.fr/france/justice/2010-08/disparus-de-l-isere-trois-dossiers-relances-5954004.html

The Family Murders. (n.d.). *The Family murders | Adelaide's most notorious unsolved serial killings*. Retrieved April 20, 2022, from https://familymurders.com/

The Namibian. (2007a, July 16). *B1 Butcher victim identified*. The Namibian. https://www.namibian.com.na/33759/archive-read/B1-Butcher-victim-identified--THE-B1-Butchers

The Namibian. (2007b, October 17). *"Butcher victim" alive*. The Namibian. https://www.namibian.com.na/38686/archive-read/Butcher-victim-alive-THE-dismembered-human

The Namibian. (2008, April 29). *B-1 Butcher: DNA evidence in spotlight*. The Namibian. https://www.namibian.com.na/40811/archive-read/B-1-Butcher-DNA-evidence-in-spotlight-REPORTS

The Oakland County Child Killer -- Case background. (2021, February 19). WDIV. https://www.clickondetroit.com/news/2019/02/01/the-oakland-county-child-killer-case-background/

Thompson, J. (2016, June 3). *Łódź: the fairy tale city you can't pronounce*. The Telegraph. https://www.telegraph.co.uk/travel/destinations/europe/articles/europe-forgotten-fairy-tale-cities/

Timeline - forensic DNA. (2019). Forensicdna.com. http://www.forensicdna.com/timeline.html

Trickey, E. (2014, June 19). *Solving the Cleveland Torso murders*. Clevelandmagazine.com. https://www.clevelandmagazine.com/in-the-cle/the-read/articles/case-closed-

Tron, G. (2021, February 19). *Who were the 4 women murdered by "The Atlantic City Serial Killer?"* Oxygen Official Site. https://www.oxygen.com/true-crime-buzz/atlantic-city-serial-killer-murdered-4-women-in-2006

Van Sambeck, B. (2021, February 5). *Who were the Colonial Parkway murder victims? 8 young people all killed in Virginia within 4 years*. Oxygen Official Site. https://www.oxygen.com/lovers-lane-murders/crime-news/who-were-the-colonial-parkway-murder-victims

Vrchoticky, N. (2021, March 24). *The untold truth of the Vending Machine Killer*. Grunge.com. https://www.grunge.com/364109/the-untold-truth-of-the-vending-machine-killer/

White, N. (2019, September 15). *Gay leader reveals the inner workings of "The Family" sex abuse ring*. Mail Online. https://www.dailymail.co.uk/news/article-7465455/Gay-leader-Lewis-Turtur-reveals-inner-workings-Family-sex-abuse-ring.html

Winchester, H., & Clarke, K. (2021, February 19). *Family of victim in Oakland County Child Killer case speaks out 45 years later*. WDIV. https://www.clickondetroit.com/news/local/2021/02/19/family-of-victim-in-oakland-county-child-killer-case-speaks-out-45-years-later/

Wizner, B. (2010, April 11). *Seria zabójstw wstrząsnęła Polską. Homo-killer wciąż na wolności*. Na Sygnale. https://www.nasygnale.pl/seria-zabojstw-wstrzasnela-polska-homo-killer-wciaz-na-wolnosci/

ZHOU, Q., KAN, B., JIAN, X., ZHANG, W., LIU, H., & ZHANG, Z. (2013). Paraquat poisoning by skin absorption: Two case reports and a literature review. *Experimental and Therapeutic Medicine*, 6(6), 1504–1506. https://doi.org/10.3892/etm.2013.1320

IMAGE REFERENCES

Beaufort, A. (2021, March 8). *Distant canal bridge with reflection*. [Image]. Unsplash. https://unsplash.com/photos/hPe7yIduDX8

Cross, L. (2022, January 9). *Free gray image*. [Image]. Unsplash. https://unsplash.com/photos/Y641G0Rrstw

Gore, T. (2019, September 4). *The city*. [Image]. Unsplash. https://unsplash.com/photos/ncY75h9FWxc

Herron, D. (2021, February 5). *Brown field under blue sky*. [Image]. Unsplash. https://unsplash.com/photos/Y5Lr_Pz7HPY

Jarrett, K. (2018, February 27). *Ferris wheel at daytime*. [Image]. Unsplash. https://unsplash.com/photos/gnTAgDzh_9k

Lovaski, R. (2020, June 3). *Grayscale photo of topless woman*. [Image]. Unsplash. https://unsplash.com/photos/Lw-ahUKYhiY

Marsan, P. (2021, April 5). *Two police men in uniform standing on road during daytime*. [Image]. Unsplash. https://unsplash.com/photos/6RB9opoO_ao

Raethel, H. (2018, January 15). *Human x-ray result chart*. [Image]. Unsplash. https://unsplash.com/photos/ouyjDk-KdfY

Rodriquez, T. (2019, June 20). *Silhouette of person near window glass*. [Image]. Unsplash. https://unsplash.com/photos/K15yk8-CC4A

Rosenke, G. (2020, February 11). *Person in red jacket and blue pants sitting on snow-covered ground*. [Image]. Unsplash. https://unsplash.com/photos/7qE8zIyNSKI

rozentuzjazmowany photography. (2020, May 11). *Łódź, Piotrkowska*. [Image]. Unsplash. https://unsplash.com/photos/BnYKvPqKCWY

Schimmeck, A. (2020, November 10). *Environmental pollution*. [Image]. Unsplash. https://unsplash.com/photos/YpOhhVGPkyQ

Scofield, W. (2018, February 7). *Vintage surgical tools*. [Image]. Unsplash. https://unsplash.com/photos/TjfQR3JgGG8

Spiske, M. (2018, December 10). *Gray and brown slide*. [Image]. Unsplash. https://unsplash.com/photos/zXP9H9umE4s

Tanabose, G. (2021, October 31). *Free South Australia image*. [Image]. Unsplash. https://unsplash.com/photos/XXhVLWDM9WQ

Thomas, M. (2020, March 29). *Man sitting alone in paradise*. [Image]. Unsplash. https://unsplash.com/photos/HnT7Pv7EO3E

Thonne, L. (2019, January 7). [Image]. *Silhouette of people standing in front of commercial chillers*. [Image]. Unsplash. https://unsplash.com/photos/dnvBOzKlWsU

Urbanek, P. (2021, May 14). *Black metal pipe on brown wooden table*. [Image]. Unsplash. https://unsplash.com/photos/evnc1Qvxphk

Winegeart, K. (2020, September 16). *Grayscale photo of ceramic mugs with coffee photo*. [Image]. Unsplash. https://unsplash.com/photos/HCG9gx422gE

www.ingramcontent.com/pod-product-compliance
Ingram Content Group UK Ltd.
Pitfield, Milton Keynes, MK11 3LW, UK
UKHW041324200725
6977UKWH00021B/158